M000298265

Reality Press
An imprint of Reality Entertainment, Inc.

important medical disclaimer

under no circumstances is the author advocating to readers the use of trance states of-mind without the guidance of a licensed mental health caregiver to help you integrate the insights revealed concerning your own unique life, death, and rebirth cycle. please refer to the guidelines of psychiatrist stan grof, m.d. given in his book psychology of the future, and to the international transpersonal association. (see www.holotropic.com)

Written by O.H. Krill
Book design and illustrations by John Malloy www.johnmalloy.net

REALITY ENTERTAINMENT
POB 91, Foresthill CA 95631
ph-530-367-5389 fx-530-367-3024
info@reality-entertainment.com
www.reality-entertainment.com

Printed in the United States of America

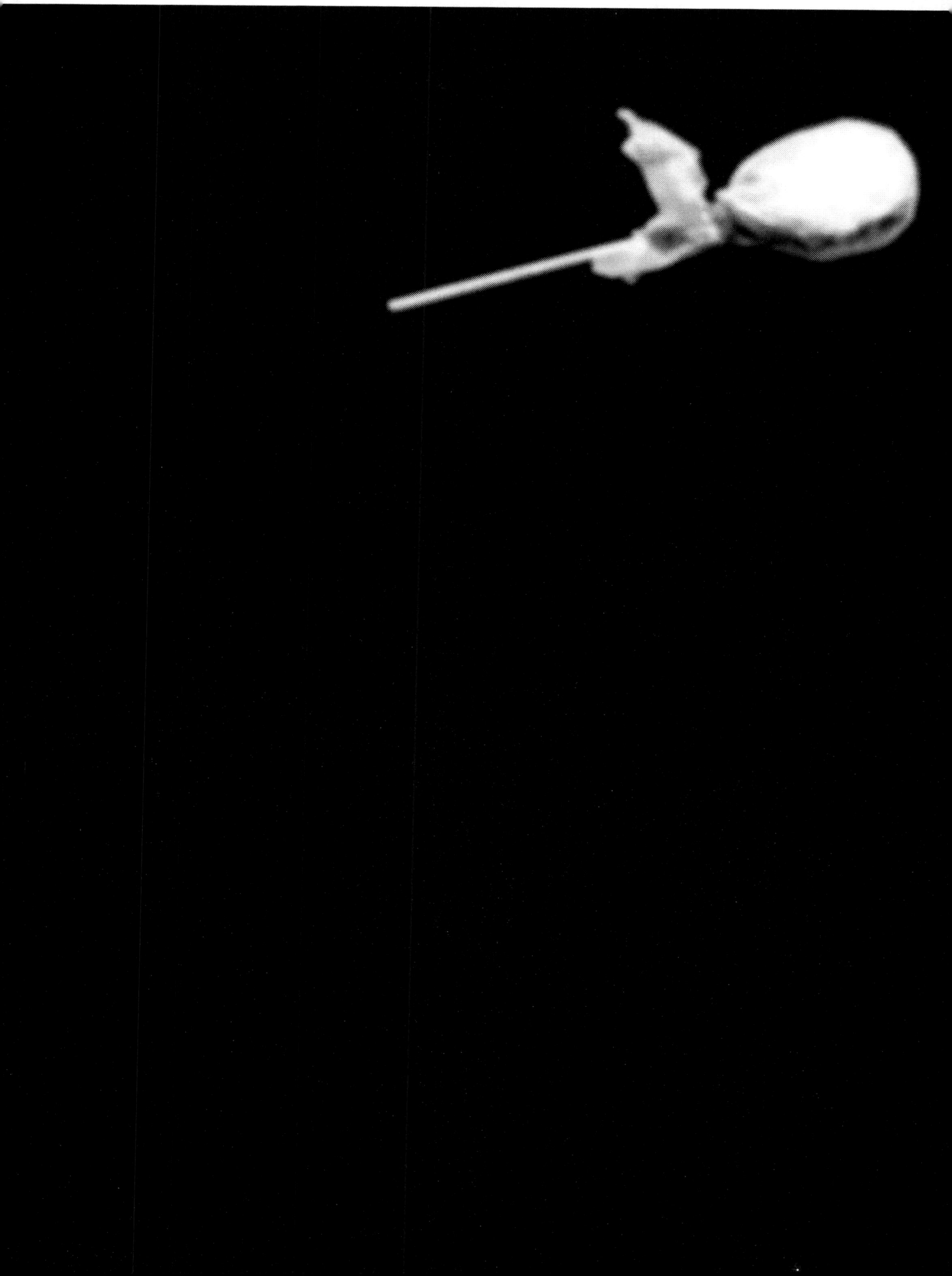

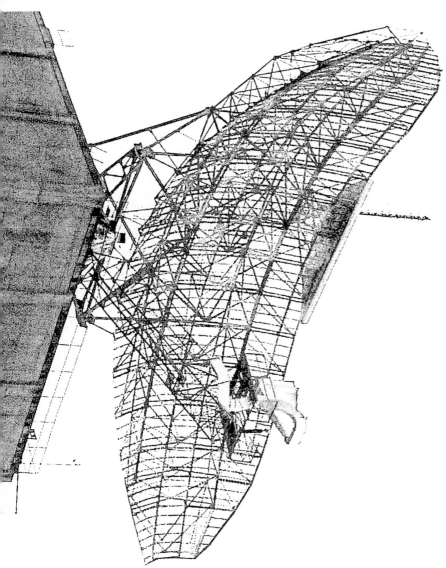

"There is only mystery left... the rest of it doesnt really matter".
Someone told me that Nikola Tesla said this or something like this upon his leaving the earthly
plane. The world would not be as it is without Tesla yet only a handful of humans know this.
His research and experimentation resonate in some way with every single technological
advancement currently on the books, including the myth of what happened at Montauk
somewhere off the Atlantic shores of North America. Stories and rumors have made
it through the grapevine if you will and as I am privy to these things, I could not get it
out of mind, and increasingly so, it willed itself into creation.

I wrote this book for Nikola Tesla.

o. h. krill

"It has become appallingly obvious that our technology has exceeded our humanity."
~Albert Einstein

"Technological progress has merely provided us with more efficient means for going backwards."
~Aldous Huxley

"Technology... the knack of so arranging the world that we don't have to experience it."
~Max Frisch

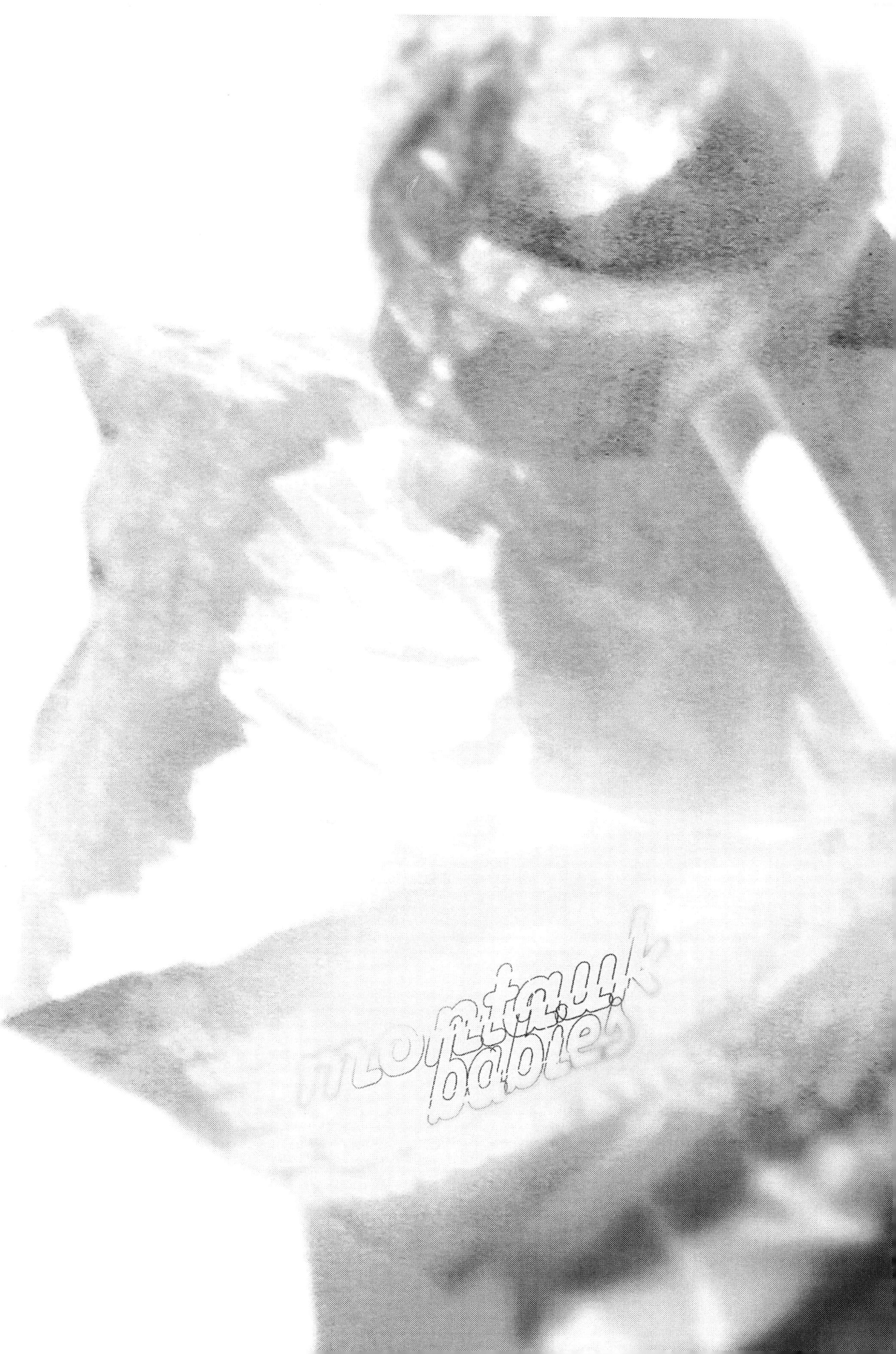
montauk
babies

chapter one

"The mortars would blow up showering red and orange shrapnel everywhere, sort of like fireworks. It was quite beautiful actually, the scenery was also really beautiful," says Al Leedskalnin. "If it weren't for all the death, I'd think differently about that place. I *re-remember*[1] it like it was yesterday. We were right in the middle of the muck... it was so damn hot... it was unbearable. We'd been livin' in the dirt for weeks when we chanced upon some ancient temples and made a bunker," Al continues, slowly shaking his head. "I hated it when the other guys would spit in there and write their names on the walls with blood... anyway, they found us out and we had to get out of there and make it to the next safe camp. We were ordered to hightail it over to the next ridge." Al pauses reflectively... "As soon as we started, the slants were all over us. It was like they were waiting."

"I remember all of us running so damn hard, sweating buckets from the humidity. We were gasping for breath, our helmets were flying off, artillery bags were getting dropped everywhere... we had no choice but to run as fast as we could to get over that ridge. Primal fear was gnawing at us and we knew that we were dead meat. We could feel our hearts pounding through our chests... we were all so incredibly ALIVE at that moment. Then... time seemed to stop. All sound ceased in that instant as we were coming to the top of that ridge. We were blinded by a stunning white light, radiating everywhere... and then, as quickly as it appeared, whatever it was just soaked back up all of its light and zipped right by us, faster than fast. That's when we saw the guys in the silver suits, this was way before that Apollo crap mind you," says Al. "These guys in platinum suits of some sort with... with hoses hanging out everywhere, come running right past us. Hell...right THROUGH us! We were just lookin' at 'em dumfounded. In fact one of 'em slammed into a private and pushed him out of the way! 'WHERE THE HELL ARE THEY GOING?' I heard one of our boys say, and here I am wondering... why are they

---

1. Re-Remember: The act of remembering an event that may or may not have actually occured.

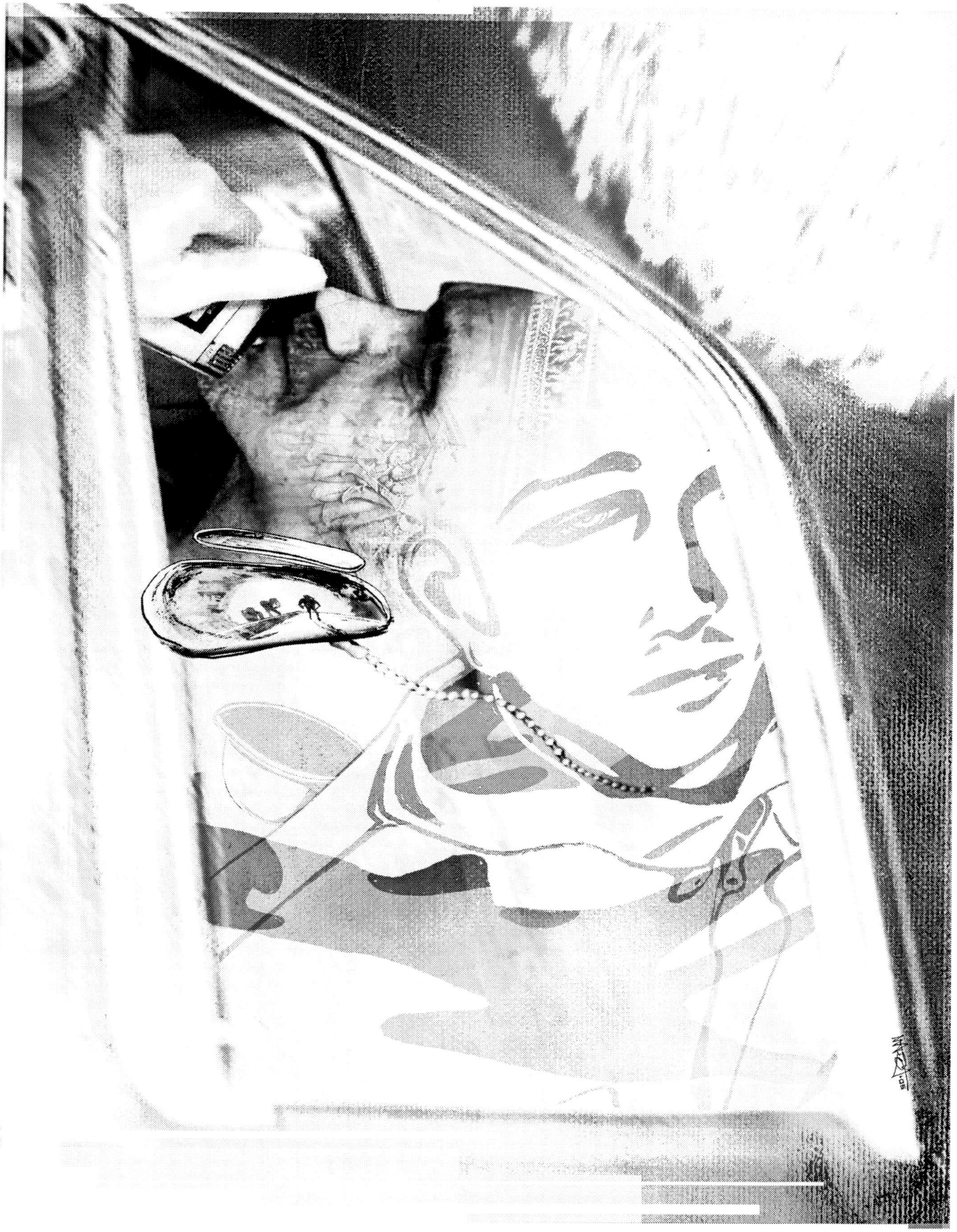

wearing helmets with gas mask looking things on 'em? By the time we did all that big thinking they were gone and our boys were RIDDLED with holes. In the mayhem we lost our footing and were easy pickin's. Anyway, I think that's when I got the stuff in my lungs..." Al pauses, turns off the hand-held tape recorder and tosses it back on the dashboard. Peabody sits next to him in the driver's seat and says, "That was good. You were able to re-remember a lot of details." "Yeah... don't get too excited. I re-remembered the last one and just repeated it, its so damn boring. The truth is, it doesn't even matter! It's all just a big feedback loop!" Al responds. "Ahhh... c'mon!" says Peabody. "Don't SAY that."

Al grabs the recorder again and says, loudly and facetiously, "On a cold and barren highway, somewhere in the middle of the American land mass, Peabody Freeman and Al Leedskalnin are driving and driving. They are traveling fast and with a purpose it would seem, but little does anyone ACTUALLY KNOW WHAT THE HELL IS REALLY GOING ON!" Al throws the recorder back on the dash. Peabody shrugs off Al's disposition with mild disgust, his jowls illuminated by the moonlight as it streaks his face through the patchy fog. Suddenly, Al notices something in the passenger rear view. Scooting up a bit, he looks concerned. He squints at the mirror for a few seconds and says, "Yep... I knew it!" as an orange orb that had previously been bobbing and languishing behind them, suddenly accelerates at an incredible speed and stops on a dime directly over the brown '74 Buick.

The Orb bumps the top of the car. "Bump! Bu-bump!" it goes, as if it to say, "I'm Watching," before veering and speeding off to the side, and quickly vanishing.

"GGGGAAADDAMMIT!" Peabody shouts as he hits the steering wheel, knocking about the papers and food wrappers on the dash. "Damn, damn, damn, DAMN!!" he says, as his psyche frays a little more. "When will it end?! WHEN?!" he cries. Al Leedskalnin simply rolls his eyes. He is too tired to get upset, truly, too tired. For him it's over. He's seen it all, and has lost track of whether he is coming or going [literally], having lived one too many lives. Peabody just shakes his head as he continues the relentless drive against the desert landscape with no apparent destination whatsoever.

They eventually pull off by a dirty coffee shop called Shonee's, one of those typical mid-western diners with the sticky yellow linoleum floor. As Peabody's massive composition completely fills his side of the booth, one of the buttons on his red shirt pops undone. He has significant, obligatory mustard stains seeping into his collar, thick black glasses that appear suctioned to his face and a pocket protector filled not only with pens, pencils and chewing gum, but interesting and delicate scientific devices. Al on the other hand could not care less, but even so, he is much more hygienic than Peabody. The food arrives and it's a bacon sandwich with fries for Peabody, hamburger patty and cottage cheese for Al. "No cream, no sugar, pleeeease." he says. Peabody waits for the waitress to leave, makes sure, then looks to Al, his worried eyes magnified through the astronaut lenses. "Have you checked the batteries? Did you rotate them the way I told you? We CANNOT lose communication!" he says, with a twinge of urgency and a loud whisper. Al nods and methodically lowers his head to take a bite of his usual bland (yet easily digestible) food. Peabody takes a bite with bacon hanging out of the side of his mouth and mumbles, "The schedule... mmph... eh-eh... slorp... is only getting... mphl... WORSE! I... grgl..." He pauses when he hears a strange electronic sound emitting from beneath the table. Al removes an egg shaped device out of his moderately weathered suit coat as Peabody waits nervously in limbo for the foreboding message. Al flips open the device with one hand and musters up only a "yeah?" then nods slowly as he listens to the voice on the other end. "Look..." he says, "it's getting difficult to hide it, alright? Make-up and soot only worked in the beginning. How about a plan to bring in some of the babies?" Under the fluorescent lights, every wrinkle in Al's face becomes garishly apparent. People are alarmed by him. His pocked skin has no life left in it, a result of abnormal circumstance and years of pounding cigarettes. He also has very thick hairs on the top of his ears. Al hits the speaker function and thrusts the device in Peabody's proximity. The voice from the other side says, "WE WILL CONTINUE OUR DIRECTIVE ...A SOLUTION IS IMMINENT, STAY VECTOR.... MAY THE LIGHT SHINE ON OUR ENDEAVOUR."

Al nods and snaps down the lid of the device, looking at Peabody with an "I told you so" expression, but Peabody already knew the answer. Al returns to his black coffee as Peabody buries himself in his portable Quantum Conversion Reference Guide. Mumbling and nodding repeatedly, he almost gives the impression that he could be mentally ill, or just mentally running through exercises of vast complication that somehow comfort him.

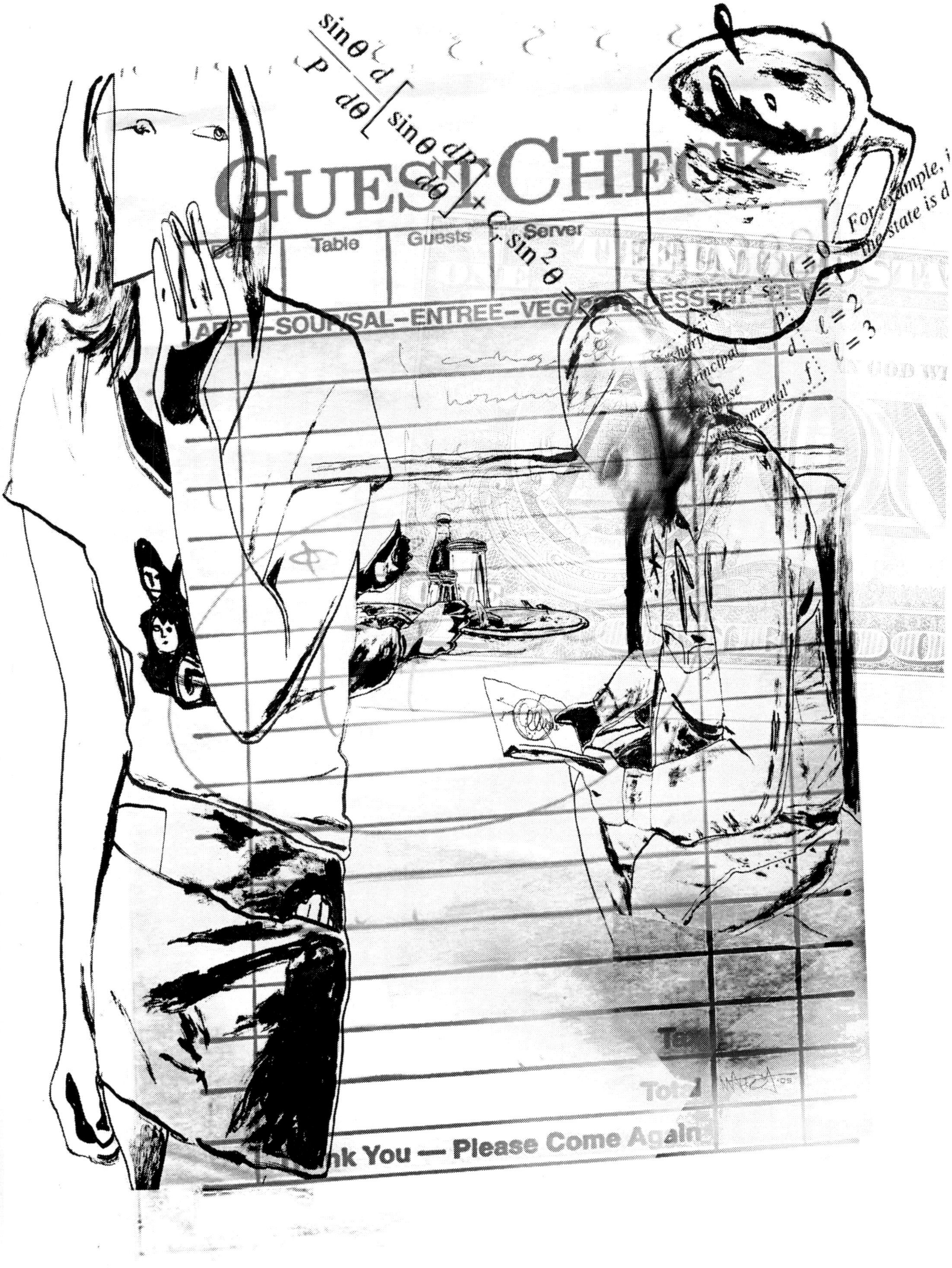
GUEST CHECK
Table
Guests
Server
APPT—SOUP/SAL—ENTREE—VEG
DESSERT
"sharp"
"principal"
"diffuse"
"fundamental"
For example,
the state is d
Total
Thank You — Please Come Again

chapter two

Deep in the Amazon rainforest, in the jungles
of Brazil, it is raining profusely. Three men
in yellow hooded raincoats are hiking with
determination, hacking vigorously at dense
vegetation with machetes to clear the way -
although it seems to grow back instantly.
There is fear in their eyes, as they nervously
look about their surroundings. Eyes are
watching them from a distance as they
move forward in the ominous jungle. They
are in a very mysterious place deep within
the continent. This is not a place where
modern man could survive, yet they seem
to know the terrain to some degree, as if
they'd been here before. Finally, they
reach a plateau where they stop and put
their tools aside. They form a single line,
all facing forward. After a short while, a
very muscular native approximately four
feet tall, emerges abruptly from a thick wall
of leaves across from them. It starts to rain
even harder, water is hammering the men, the
sound is deafening. The native is well adorned
and formidably intense, he is most definitely a
Shaman and it would appear that he has lived a
long, long time. His stone-like pupils are terrifying as
he mentally grips the group. They do not move or even think about
looking him directly in the eye as he walks around them, finally stopping to stare at Browning.
The Shaman's speech is translated blow-by-blow by one of the other men, referred to as the
"Professor". He translates by shouting loudly over the rain while another takes
his words in with a small recorder. "THERE ARE ONLY YOUR ILLUSIONS LEFT,"
he says, "THEY ARE THE FABRIC OF THIS DREAM... THE LONG DARK
SLEEP-...". The shaman makes a gesture with both of his hands pressed
together, leans his head to one side and says, "-...IS OF YOUR OWN
MAKING AND NOW THERE IS NO MORE. IT HAS REACHED
THE END."

The men are speechless
as they and the shaman
are pelted by the
thundering, violent
downpour.
The Shaman says
nothing more.

Peabody and Al pull up to the oldest Motel6 west of the Mississippi, complete with 70's shag carpet, faded brown paint, and plenty of traffic noise. They walk past a beat-up ice machine as a man walks around the corner giving them a curious, sinister glance. They progress forward a few steps when Peabody looks over his shoulder and says to Al with some contempt, "Did he look familiar? I can't even tell anymore." Al grimaces and mumbles, "yeah, I know... let's get ready. I'm fading." Peabody opens his door, gives Al his own room card and says, "I'll be at your room in 5 minutes, OK?" Al nods, still mumbling, "yeah, just be ready this time," and walks away, habitually looking up and down the hall as he inserts the plastic key. Peabody throws his coat and old thrift-store suitcase on the bed and goes to the window to reflect. He remembers happier times and daydreams of when he had his own lab and was involved in the most cutting-edge scientific research of his time. He visualizes himself walking the hallways of the old facility, with his clipboard in hand. He sees his own hand making notations as he comes upon an enclosure, turning only to find a naked man screaming in agony. The man holds on to his own arm as it starts to disintegrate right before his own eyes. "BEEP... BEEP... BEEP... BEEP..."

Peabody snaps out of his daydream, startled by the cheap plastic alarm clock that was set for 2:15 AM. He stares at it for about 7 seconds before gently turning it off, then approaches his road-worn suitcase and gently unpacks a handful of unusual, stringy metal components. Screwing two or three sections together, he grabs the complete device and puts it behind his back as if to hide it from any potential observers. Leaving his room, he scurries across the hall and knocks on Al's door. "IN!" barks Al. Peabody enters, securing the door behind him and stands directly over Al, who is stretched out horizontally on the bed. Al's suit jacket lays neatly on the chair, he has his arm extended up with the back of his hand over his forehead as if to shield himself from harmful rays. Peabody gets ready to "connect" when Al prompts "Turn it down.. it's still too loud! Damn thing! I don't want anybody calling the cops again." Peabody nods and leans down over Al, placing the device on his chest. It quickly emits a vibrating sound and a fairly loud multiple octave tone, which he adjusts down to a reasonable volume. Al writhes very slightly but endures the effects of the device for a few minutes before settling himself. Peabody looks on, holding his quantum conversion reference guide in his other hand. He squints his eyes in deep thought and after a while, looks over at Al and removes the device very routinely. Al just lays there, completely silent, as if he were dead.

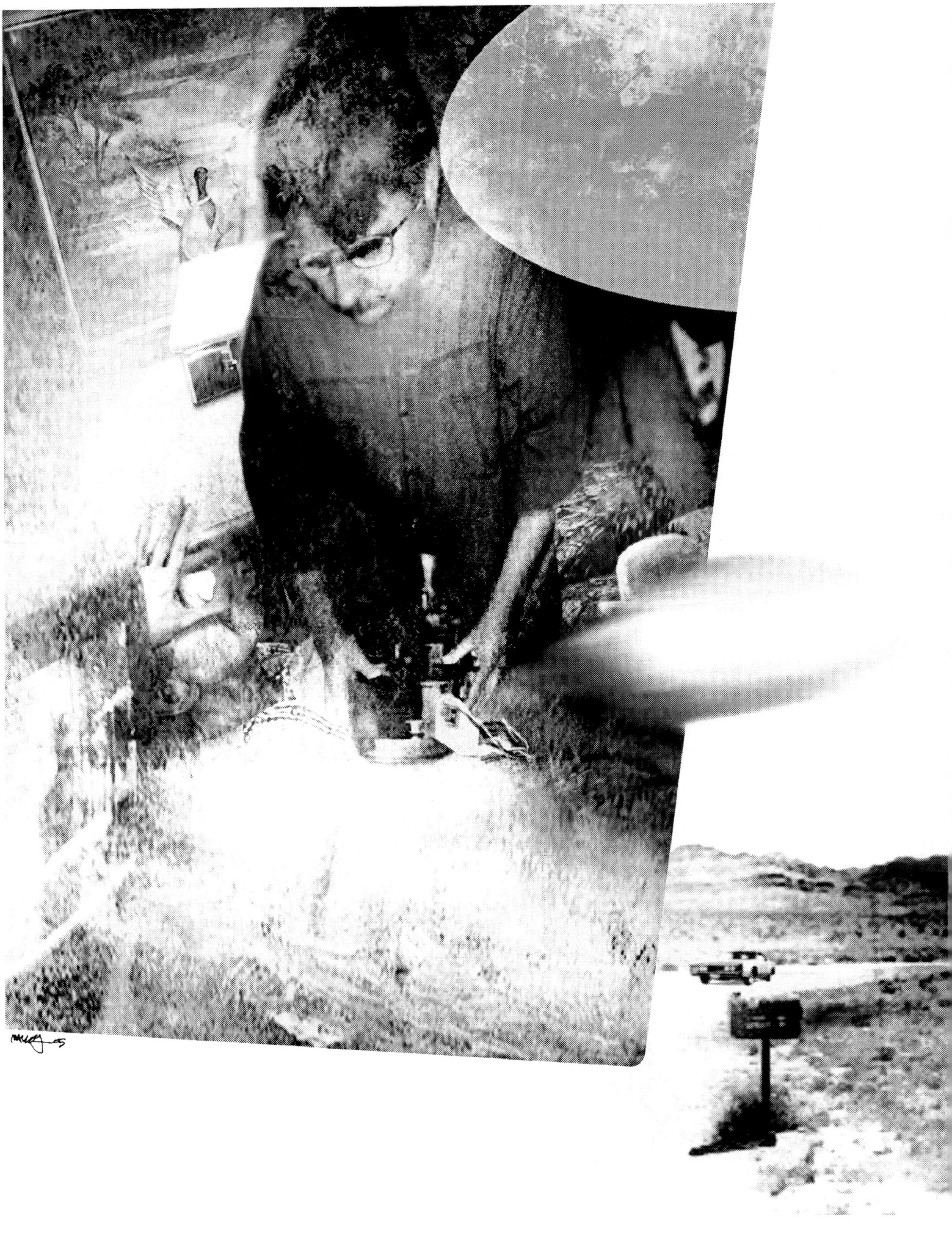

In the morning, Peabody and Al are back on the highway, driving in the blinding, merciless desert sun. Their surroundings are considerably harder on the eyes in daylight. Peabody mumbles to himself while driving intently and as always, Al stares straight out at the road. Hours later, an undefined silvery object, which they are not alarmed by at all, streaks past them leaving behind a trail of damp heat. They know it's coming for them. As this ridiculously unbelievable event occurs, the station wagon next to them veers to and fro, its tires screech and skid, finally coming to a dead stop in the middle of the road. Peabody is slightly irritated by all of this as he slows down and makes a huffy, matter-of-fact U-turn. As they pass the station wagon, they do not make contact with its bewildered passengers, and they accelerate down the road at a good clip. "Over There!" exclaims Al. Peabody pulls off the road, goes around a bend and puts the Buick in park. Dust kicks up around the vehicle, making it nearly invisible. Al immediately jumps out, barking, "Alright... stay here! I'll be back in a minute." He climbs over a small hill and disappears from sight. Peabody sits alone, bobbing up and down, squinching his eyes in mathematical contemplation for several minutes. He finally looks up to see Al coming around to the front of the car. Al hastily gets in and slams the door. "Ok," Al says, "I've got a handle on it. We're good for a minute or so. I figure it's probably gonna be Northeast of here, around noontime tomorrow". "That's good," snaps Peabody. "We need more time. I can't get around why it's so random! I can't seem to find a pattern of any sort. If we can't rely on everything I know to get us out of this, then we might as well KILL OURSELVES! If it's true... if there IS no way to stop it, even with science and logic, that would indicate that all our theories are wrong, which maybe I could handle... but not knowing how wrong? Not being able to develop a new foundation?... Makes it UNBEARABLE!" Al stares directly at Peabody as he speaks, but can't hear a word. Peabody's face goes in and out of focus, becoming pixilated, as the noises start up inside Al's head, "GJRRRK... GRRRKKKK... grrkkk..." After a moment Peabody's panic attack subsides, and he slowly becomes more visible. "C'mon kid," Al suggests, "Let's go to the ParaDice. Remember that place from the last time we were around these parts? It's better than driving around in this ass of a dust bowl."

chapter three

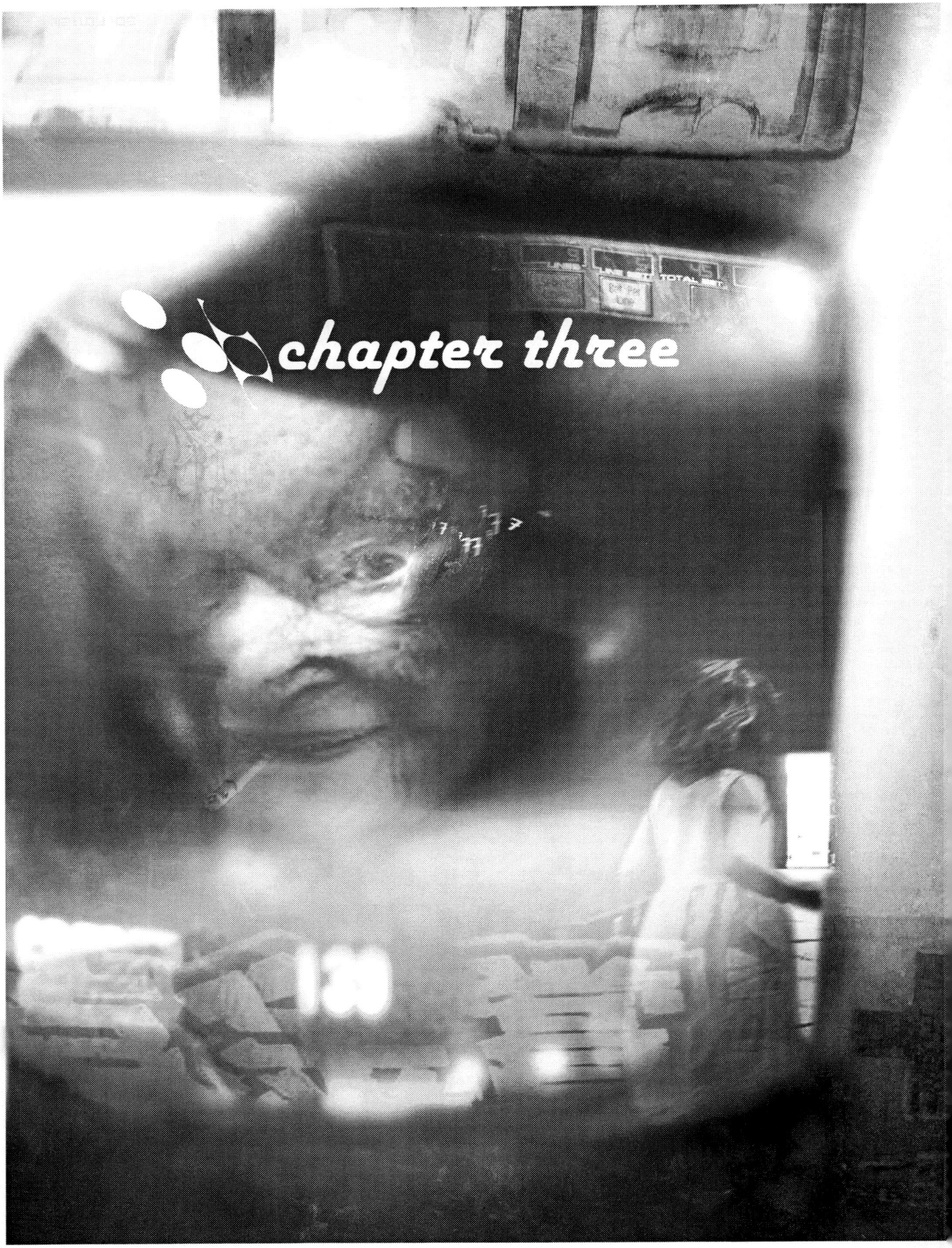

Peabody and Al pull off the road into the ParaDice Lounge, a desert roadside cocktail house. It's a quiet bar. A few hooligans in the corner are somewhat concerning, but Al and Peabody progress on regardless. Al approaches a rugged, blue-collar farmer type who's hunched over slurping a Pabst Blue Ribbon. Al senses that the man knows him somehow and sarcastically says, "How's the fields?" "Oh... slim pickin's about now," says the farmer, looking a little confused. Al takes the stool next to him while Peabody gets comfortable a few stools away in a dark corner at the end of the bar. "What's it to you anyway?" says the farmer. "Nothing to me. It's the rest of you I'm thinking about. There's some interesting stuff out there," Al says. "The rest of us? What do you mean?" the farmer asks. "Aw, forget it. Just be aware that things aren't always what they seem, that's all I'm saying," Al replies. "How 'bout we drop it and I buy you a beer?" "Fine with me," says the farmer. The barkeep rolls up with another Pabst.

In the meantime, Peabody is drawn to an emaciated, much older lady who's vigorously slamming away at the video poker game next to him. He begins watching intently as she loads in her nickels and slams the slot machine handle over and over, never dumping her 3-inch cigarette ash even once. A small girl with a blue bow tied around her head comes from the back door to light up another one for her while the old lady continues to stuff nickel after nickel, never missing a beat. The sun bleaches their corner of the bar every time the little girl comes and goes through the back exit door. Al comes over and joins Peabody, looks intently at the machine and says in a low voice so as not to be overheard, "I'm sure you're wondering why I approached that fellow while you were hiding back here. I thought he might be a clone... but he's not." Peabody can't really be bothered. His bulbous eyes are fixed on the screen next to him. Al's eye's follow his lead. When the game hits all sevens, Al hears the noises in his head, "GRRRKK... grrkkkkkk... GRRRkKKKKkkk...", which stop after a few seconds. Peabody scribbles "777" in his small, spiraled notebook.

Back on the 375, Al looks black and white against a dim color backdrop. Peabody glances over at him and begins to daydream as the punishing sun beats the worn leather interior of the Buick. He drifts off and sees Al in a cold, riveted, bullet-gray room. Al is quarantined, holding his fuzzy, out-of-focus arm in front of him. Peabody examines him through a small window in the door. Pulling back from the window, he's approached by a high-ranking military officer walking down the hall who asks, "Full body?" "No, just one arm right now. Be able to circulate him soon," says Peabody. "Right," replies the officer, as he continues down the hallway, the heels of his shoes rhythmically tapping the cold floor. Peabody jerks back to the present when Al asks to be driven to the spot, as if prompted by an unseen force. When they get there, Al immediately gets out of the car and starts walking straight to the highest point in the sand. It's windy and dusty, his jacket flaps are rustling wildly while Peabody towers outside the car, patiently waiting and watching. They're both looking for something. Neither is sure exactly what, but something that only they could recognize after all this time together. They are very close to the old mailbox road, where so many have disappeared. They aren't worried for themselves though. They know they are far too valuable a commodity.

When they see some atmospheric activity emanating from the West, their curiosity is peaked as the clouds slowly move closer to them. They're both completely engaged, standing on the tips of their toes staring out at the emerging group of clouds which are growing bigger and moving even faster toward them. The ground starts to become a little greener, grasses start to pop through the tough desert soil and a blanket of damp humidity descends over the area. Peabody is squinting and blinking from the dew accumulating on his eyeglasses and Al's stare becomes even more stern than usual, as if the clouds would disappear if he took his eyes off of them, even for a second. After several minutes, Al looks back to Peabody and says, "There's still a chance Freeman... there's still a chance." Peabody sighs, given a brief second of relief.

Back at the Motel6, at the farthest end of the complex, on the highest floor, they rendezvous in Al's room again. Al has the device strapped to his chest. The slightly moldy room smells of cigarettes, Al grimaces a little while Peabody is calibrating the device, gargling, "DAMN SMOKERS! This life is down-right uncivilized!" "Al, you used to smoke like a chimney," retorts Peabody. "Don't be a hypocrite." "That's because we didn't know jack in those days kid. Hell, if you didn't smoke you were a sissy! That goes double for eatin' bacon too!" barks Al. Peabody pleads, "Let's just do this. We need to be on our toes tomorrow." Al closes his eyes and lies still. Peabody monitors the device, simultaneously running algorithms on his Texas Instruments calculator, always searching for an equation that might give them some peace.

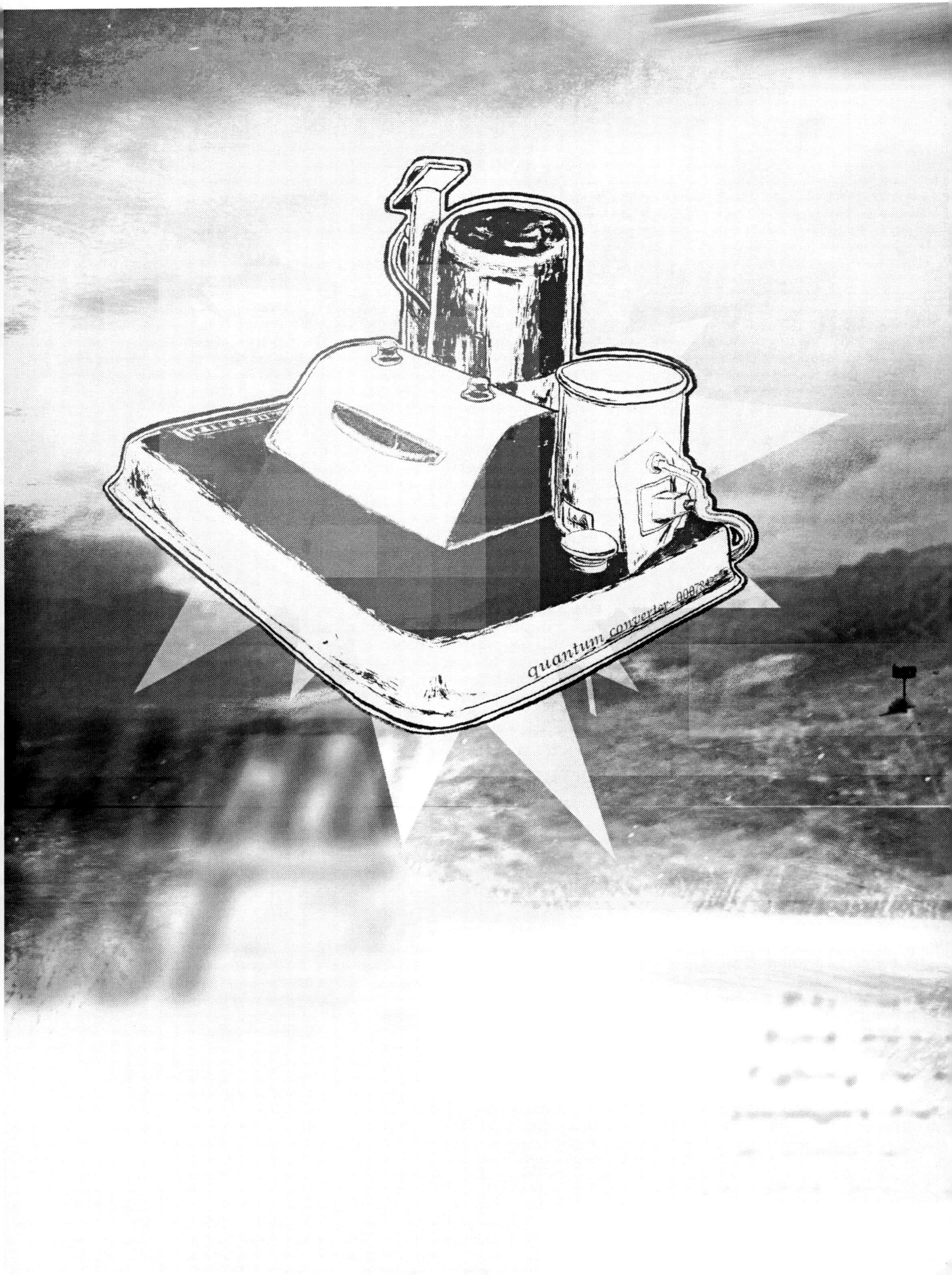
quantum converter

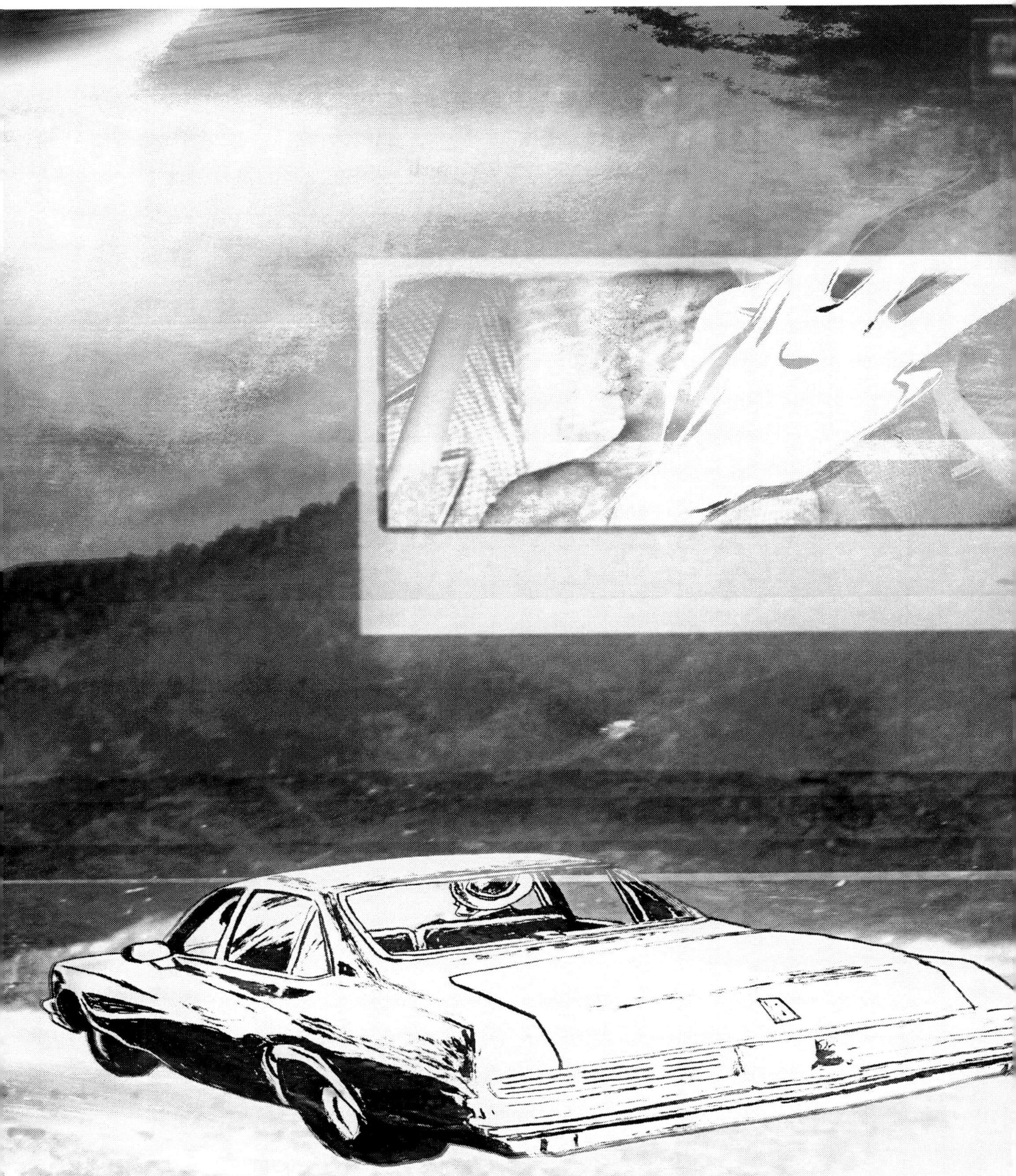

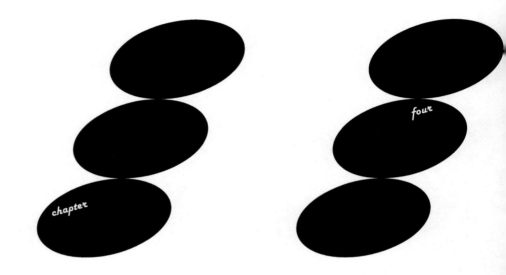

chapter four

As they emerge out of the rain-drenched forest, the three men in yellow raincoats get into a small submersible located at the edge of a vast river. "Why don't we just airlift? I'm tired of the daylong hikes every time we do this," says Colonel Ramsey, the most militant of the trio. Browning. He's the Navy's *RV*[1] top gun, and the youngest of the group. Browning responds, "The Shaman doesn't like it... says it angers the elementals or something." "Oh THAT makes sense!" barks Ramsey in a facetious and sour tone. Browning draws their attention with his somber mood, saying, "I really don't know if we will be doing this again. Usually, we get a vital piece of insight but... that was pretty damn bleak." There is a profound silence as each of them

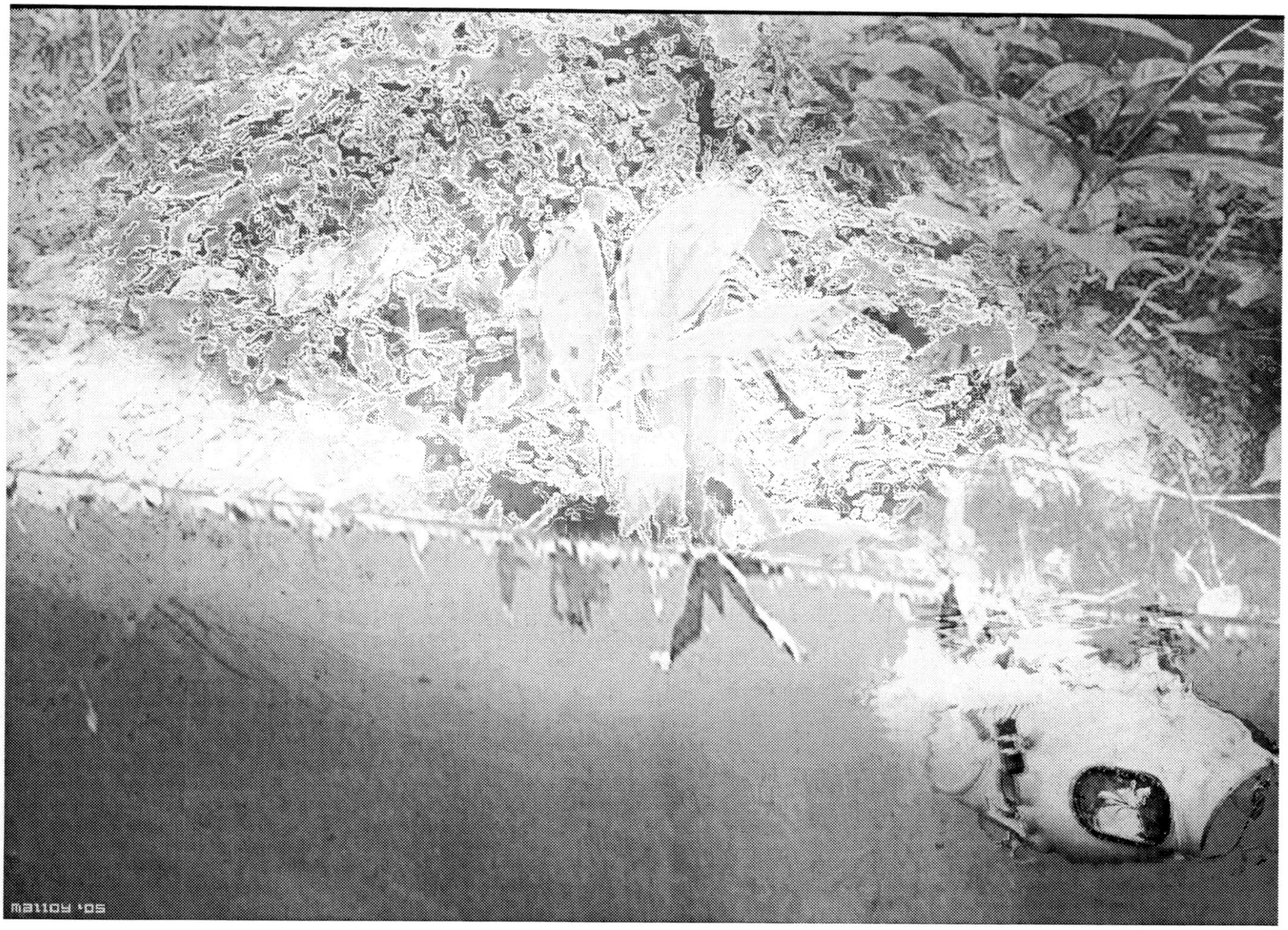
malloy '05

thinks of their friends and loved ones. Reflecting, the professor breaks the silence and says, "You might not believe this, but I heard that shortly after the technology began disseminating, Howard Hughes was somehow in communication with the Shaman. He was one of the first to speak with him, probably the first. He used the Shaman to better understand the consequences of his own experiments, which picked up right where the Nazis left off. He was opening inter-dimensional doors that could not be closed. He was an amazing man, far ahead of his time... While everyone thought he was working on the Spruce Goose, he was right here, in the Amazon, the source of all life... If people only knew what he was ultimately trying to do... but of course, he went insane like they all did in the beginning."

1. RV: [Remote Viewing] ESP information identifying a physical location or object at a distance from the receiver. Sometimes used synonymously with clairvoyance and could involve multiple ESP capacities [i.e. telepathy or precognition].

"Quick, I'm re-remembering!" shouts Al, as he experiences his first feedback loop of the day, snatching the recorder from the dashboard. "The current reality continues to mask the... the... banality of existence with false EXUBERANCE, compelled by technology to the... the... deterioration of the *LOGOS*[1]!" He says this in a disembodied robotic voice, then collapses back into the passenger seat. Peabody hardly flinches. He just looks over at Al and continues to drive, recalling when he and Al were on different sides of the fence, but somehow they ulti-mately formed a certain kind of bond. Drifting off, Peabody remembers the sessions in the 70's room. That's what it's called now anyway, now that it's infamous in UFO conspiracy circles and the like. In one session, Al is ordered to give Peabody information telepathically, as part of a military propelled astral directive that he has been assigned to. The room is wallpapered with striking, multi-colored geodesic patterns. This is where Al has time trav-eled and has had profound realizations that have changed him forever. He has seen more than one could possibly endure without total collapse and is still somehow able to function and perform his directives. From the small window of the 70's room, Peabody recalls seeing a shiny metallic object descending slowly, blocking out the light for a few seconds, then passing. He thinks to himself, "Did it land right outside?" Peabody's brow contorts, expressing fear and even terror . "Is something outside? Is it real?" he worries, completely hypnotized. "Outside the window? Did something just happen?" he says softly, a few more times.

I. LOGOS: The light that gives one *gnosis,* or intuition of spiritual truths, via general communication and interconnectedness. It is, in essence, *the Christ* [not to be confused with Jesus], and uses the same energy that gives form to thoughts and ideas, as through words. This knowledge is passed on through words in this world. It gives one guidance by way of a heightened ability to *see* and comprehend.

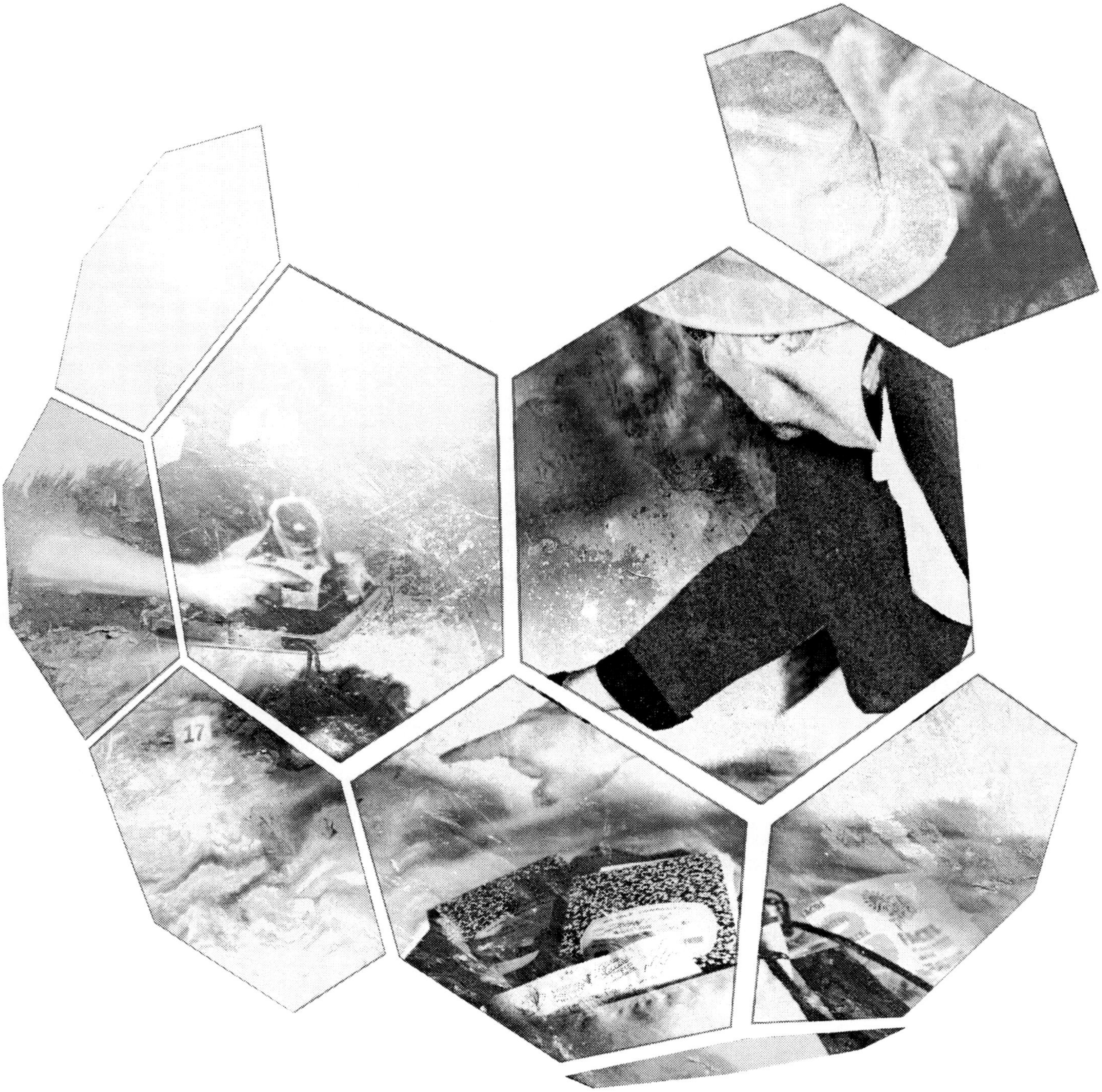
17

Al finally comes to in the Buick, looking like he's got a lost weekend hangover. He mutters, "Anything new?" "No, nothing new," says Peabody, "Wasn't important anyway, just a miss-channel. I can see the weather changing up ahead past the last town and I'm getting a good *orgonomic*[1] reading. I think we're here. It's really close to the first hole we had in this area, actually." Al perks up and says, "Yeah, I can feel it. Pull over just past that rise."

They continue on and eventually pull off the highway. As they progress toward their destination, the atmosphere becomes more overcast, gray, and damp. They stop, get out of the Buick and look around with some trepidation. Suddenly Al proceeds swiftly in a straight line toward the mountains, then slows down and begins to step very cautiously as if he's tracking something. His senses are all very focused as he starts and stops, starts and stops, pauses again, and abruptly barks, "**HERE FREEMAN! RIGHT HERE!**" He points to the spot and in that instant, **FWOOOOSH!!!** A beaming ball of light bursts out of the ground, jetting through a dense patch of desert shrubbery next to Al's foot. It's moving very fast (you'd miss it if you were to blink 3 times quickly) and it looks like a nuclear baseball, arching with bolts of electricity and phosphorescent subatomic particles. As fast as it happens, Peabody is at the spot where it emerged. He barrels on over and takes out an orange table marker that he took from Del Taco on a recent lunch break and places it next to the hole. Al, still looking up at the sky, says," Who knows where it'll come down? It's getting a lot harder to tell... hell, it could come down in Saigon for all we know." "I highly doubt THAT!" says Peabody, "If anything it'll be within 2 miles and with some luck we'll get exact coordinates from the RV guys. We've been doing good lately." "Yeah... real good," smirks Al facetiously, as he forcefully points to the hole. Peabody quickly re-focuses his attention as he takes the same device he uses on Al out of his duffle bag. After habitually securing the items in his pocket protector, he turns a few small knobs and places the device on the ground next to the hole. The small hole still has some smoke emanating from it. Peabody turns on the device and steps back as the hole quickly fills itself in. It would appear the device works via some sort of sympathetic frequency, a kind of vibrational energy. Peabody picks up the device and cries," Thank you *TESLA*[2]!" in a soft voice, then blows a few grains of sand off the device and starts back for the car with Al lagging behind.

As they pull up to the Roy Rogers, the bright lights and loud colors unsettle Al. He grimaces as he looks at his surroundings. Even with his huge wraparound sunshields on he can barely tolerate the process. The sound of the intercom and the voice on the other side saying, "We have a super-size combo available," is unbearable. Peabody pays with his black ops credit card that says Chemical Bank. Then they're back on the road as Peabody hoovers his egg sandwiches, crumpling the wrappers and throwing them into the backseat of the Buick. Al doesn't eat much and certainly can't today. He stares ahead as his vision goes in and out of focus and the sound in his head starts up again,
"GJRRRRKK... GRRRKKKK... kkkggggrrrrrrr..."

1. ORGONE: An alleged type of "primordial cosmic energy" discovered by Wilhelm Reich [1897-1957], an Austrian-born medical doctor, psychiatrist, and Freudian psychoanalyst. Among other things, Reich claimed that it was the 'creative force in nature', and the basis of the human libido.
2. TESLA: a. A unit of magnetic flux density equal yo one *weber* per square meter. b. [Nikola Tesla 1856-1943] Serbian-born U.S. inventor and electrical engineer, responsible for discovering neon tubes, the principles of the A/C current, and inventing the first alternating current induction motor, the Tesla Coil, and several types of oscillators.

chapter five

Browning became the top man by accident. He was hit by a mortar shell in the Gulf War, sustaining several lacerations and a great deal of shrapnel to the head and brain. Surgeons worked for hours to clean him up but just couldn't get it all. After some weeks of recuperation, he realized that he could remember all the numbers in his small phone book without looking. It also occurred to him that he was able to add, subtract and multiply large numbers effortlessly in his head. Considering that he barely graduated high school and was listening to a Slipknot CD when he was gunned down, this was no small feat. Unfortunately, this epiphany soured. Browning began getting very nervous and fearful as he was closely monitored for the next several weeks. Gradually, it became apparent that Browning could do more, much more. He told the ward shrink that he could leave his body at will, the only problem was getting back. He said he could go just about anywhere and would disembody on a regular basis, flying in and out of the huge AC vents of the facility when he couldn't sleep. When he realized he could "be" anywhere at anytime, it really rattled him, probably just because of the enormity of this realization in and of itself. But because he was a soldier, the Navy was apt to put him through ridiculous and endless tests that in the end, concluded nothing. That's when they consulted the Montauk Division, which was known for sleep deprivation and isolation experiments, as well as de-molecularizing people by accident. When Colonel Ramsey, the then director for project Window Shade asked Browning "If you can travel anywhere, anytime, then why don't you go to the edge of the Solar System and tell us about the planet Saturn, tell me what the surface looks like?" Browning would never be the same.

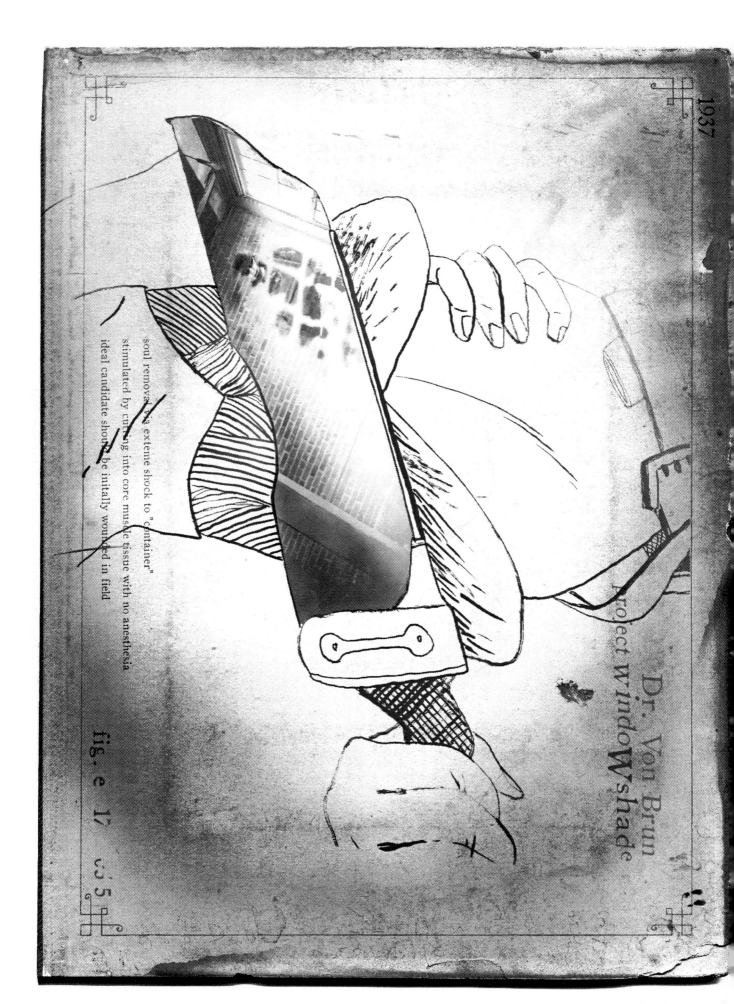

1937

Dr. Von Brun

project Window shade

soul removal via extreme shock to "container"
stimulated by cutting into core muscle tissue with no anesthesia
ideal candidate should be initially wounded in field

fig. e 17 & 5

Several days later, Al and Peabody have located a large looming web of clouds that appear to be moving toward the Rhinestone Casino, a hot spot of depravity on the outskirts where the *chicken farms*[1] are. They roll around to the back and enter through a service entrance. Al catches the door as a prep cook leaves the building and enters the kitchen with a certain confidence. They're not challenged, as it seems the kitchen staff is under the impression that they're health inspectors. Al walks about swiftly, scoping out the kitchen area, even going by the freezers to report, "Not here," then moves out to the dining area, until

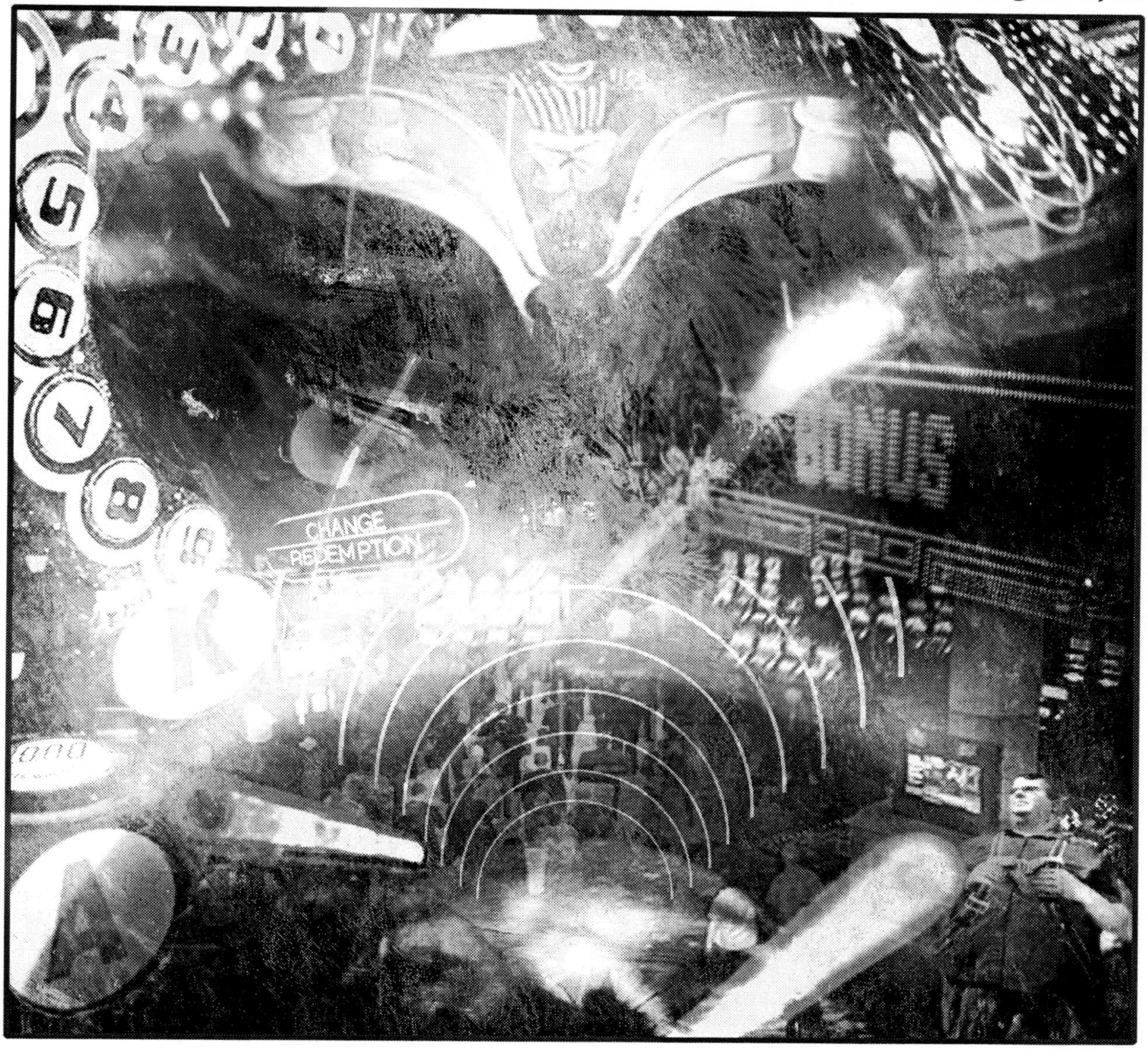
CHANGE
REDEMPTION

he arrives at the casino floor. Peabody is close in tow with his black duffle bag. He's trying, with some success, to be as anonymous as possible. The gambling area is packed with people. The walkways are congested with gambling retirees and Marlboro huffing hopefuls from the surrounding trailer parks. Al passes the Lucky 7 silver dollar machine, stops abruptly and then backs up. He starts looking up at the ceiling and rotates himself clockwise in a full circle, wincing in concentration. Finally, he walks exactly two more steps and says in a low voice, "Here... right here." Peabody nods. They stare at each other for a brief moment. They both know it's easiest and best to say nothing and not alarm the people. They just hope that

1. CHICKEN FARM: An estabilshment not prohibited under federal or state law to provide services of ill repute primarily to white males ranging from 18-43 years of age.

no one steps over that spot, when suddenly, FWWOOOOSSH!!! There's a slight ricochet sound as the arching orb is visible for a half second. The sound is audible but amazingly not loud enough to override the cacophonous clang of the casino. The patrons keep squandering their pensions and ordering watered-down mixed drinks. It's so loud you couldn't hear 100 witches scream and the accident is so precise that there's hardly any debris at all. Peabody bends down to "tie his shoe lace" with Al standing by him in such a way as to give him added room as he hulks over the hole, which is more or less covered by foot-long flaps of red and gold carpet. Peabody sets down the device, selects a few settings, and triggers it. The hole fills itself up *almost* instantly. He hasn't said anything to Al, but he knows it's expanding. He's been calibrating the device higher for each successive accident to compensate for this. Finally, Peabody gets up, shakes his head in disgust and says, "There's got to be a better way, I need to get my lab back!" Al shrugs and bitterly asks "Why bother? We should skip on the whole damn thing and go to Acapulco. Screw it!" They quickly head for the lobby area and separate into the masses. They exit different doors, each making a beeline to the parking lot. Reconvening at the Buick, Peabody tries to sooth Al by saying, "It's just that I can't stand only being able to put a band-aid on the problem is all...." "YOU'VE HAD PLENTY OF CHANCES!" snaps Al, "Stay vector, Freeman! Anything can happen. NOW GET US OUT OF HERE!"

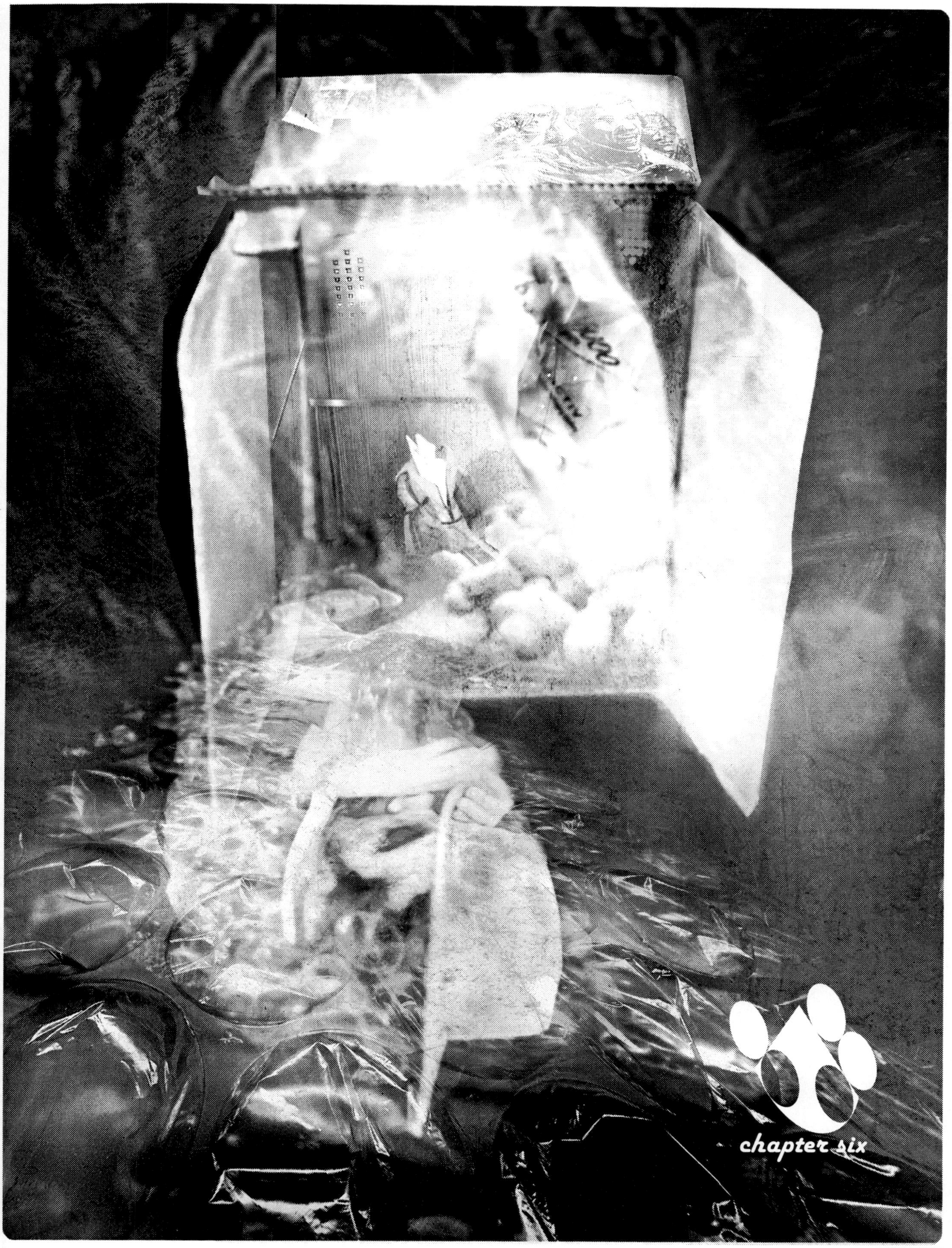
chapter six

malloy'05

Nine days later, at a different Motel6 closer to town, Peabody and Al are going down an elevator that creaks with the sounds of an ailing pulley system. Inside the wood-paneled compartment there's a loud silence between them. Peabody gives Al a sort of once-over and says, "Looks good... really." It in fact does seem that Al has a little more color to his face than before, but he's mildly perturbed with Peabody as he continues to look forward. "It does!" urges Peabody in a further attempt to console Al. Al is something of a human time bomb. His body has a tendency not to stay together for very long. Ever since he was dematerialized several times into former bodies, the physical essence of Al has been prone to pull apart. Peabody is not directly responsible for this, but understands the problem better than anyone on earth.

They've learned to look for coincidences and synchronicities, not only to protect themselves, but to look for clues to assist them in their agenda. Part of the reason Al is in the field is because he is in-tune with aliens in a way that no one else really can be. He knows that they cannot get directly involved but they can assist by delivering information by pure thought rather than with words, just like all of their mechanisms. According to Al, they are so evolved that they think without making thoughts. They are far beyond the limitations of language or semantics and don't use "words". The mental picture they portray when referring to humans is akin to a container or box, they suggest that humans are simply existing in boxes. Al is extremely sensitive to these pure thoughts and is one of only a few who can not only receive them, but can cope with their implications. Most with these abilities have not made it as far as Al. Regardless, he and Peabody are forced to endure accident duty whether they like it or not. Once you're in the programs, your ALWAYS in the programs. They are both aware that humanity is in very deep trouble and that a catastrophe of some sort is imminent. And even though they have lost everything, they hang on to the hope that they can somehow relinquish themselves of this burden they have endured for so long, envying the lives that most humans have taken for granted.

As soon as they get out of the elevator, they are descended upon by a small mob of sci-fi freaks. "Seems they've found us!" snaps Al. "Must be a convention in town, that could mean something," says Peabody. "Uh huh," Al murmurs, staring forward as he proceeds to the Buick, followed by several enterprising geeks. One of them has a recorder and urges, "Sir, are you also Ned Christy? And are you also William Pennington? Is this true? We know who you are. It's all over the boards and forums. What happened at Montauk, Mr. Leedskalnin?" "What!? Are you a reporter?! For Chrissakes, kid. You don't want to know the half of it. Go back to your damn convention !!" "The convention isn't until next week. We're camping out by the old mailbox road hoping to see something," the geek replies. "Awwwww, now that's stupid kid," Al says. "Plain stupid! Go home. You should ALL just go home!" Peabody fires up the Buick as Al slips through the passenger door, hanging on to his black derby. They quickly drive away from the geeks out onto the flat, endless, asphalt parking lot and finally get back onto a two-lane highway heading north for no apparent reason. Sometimes they just need to drive... until they are too tired, or until something happens.

"DUMB PUNKS!" says Al, disgruntled. "Come on Al. You'd be doing the same thing if you were them. There have been so many phenomena since the 50's that it's all bound to come to a head. Those kids are just trying to figure it all out." "Never should have happened!" fires Al. "We should have never brought those prissy Occult Nazi bastards over here!" "Whatever Al," pipes Peabody.

chapter 7

"Al, do you remember that safe feeling? You were around in the 60's in some form right?" Peabody continues. "My dad once told us that he last remembered that safe feeling in the early 60's... that's when you'd have big gatherings with all the people in the neighborhood, called block parties. Pretty amazing concept. He said everyone knew everyone else and they all helped each other out, back when life was still simple, even before credit cards." "Oh Bosh! They had credit cards in the 60's alright but of course it was all just getting started around then," Al retorts. "The IBM guys took the ball and really ran with it when nobody else would. Hell, there would have never been the 'new economy' if it wasn't for those bastards, but even they really had no idea of the implications." There's a silence between them as they drive on. Al drifts into re-remembering and a smug smile emerges on his face. He looks like he's in a trance when this happens. He remembers hanging out with his Army chums at a bar by the docks smoking Lucky Strikes back when you rolled the pack up in your shirt sleeve so it poked out your shoulder. Even though they were in the middle of World War II, life and times were still much simpler than they would ever be again. Al or, at that time Ned Christy, is having a merry time drinking and guffawing, really whooping it up with his compadres, when suddenly a blue arch flashes in his arm. He drops his Blue Ribbon, which explodes on the floor as he clutches the arm, screaming in pain. He further flashes back to the incident that he and the others had put away deep in the recesses of their minds. The blue arch that sent most of them to the funny farm forever, or what was left of them anyway. Al winces shaking his head back and forth. "Gzzzzz... Grrrrrk...Grrrkkkkkkk" "AL! AL! it's OK! AL!" Peabody yells. "Grrrrrrrrrhhhhnnnnn......." Al grumbles, finally coming out of it. He reaches for the tape recorder, says, "GODDAMN FEEDBACK LOOP!" and throws it back on the dash.

As they continue to drive accident duty, it seems they barely pass one vehicle every hour when Al notices a fuzzy brown football shaped object that is about 300 yards away, directly outside Peabody's window. Al watches it for a few seconds and yells, "9 o'clock Freeman!" Peabody jerks to look and it disappears. "Uh huh," scowls Al, "Very strange indeed... never seen THAT before. We've got us a new bogey!" The object re-appears on Al's side. Peabody catches it out the corner of his eye. "3 o'clock! It's back!" he shouts. The object appears and re-appears for several minutes. His curiosity peaked, Peabody slowly takes his foot off the gas, until they reach 30 mph. Amazingly enough, the object slows with them. He then speeds up to approximately 90 mph and again it tracks right along with them. The Buick's got a 396 and can do more no problem. Like all things mechanical, Peabody knows engines too. They continue this cat and mouse scenario for another 10 minutes, until finally Al exclaims, "TO HELL WITH IT! PULL OVER! GET READY WITH SOME ORGONE JUST IN CASE!" Peabody pulls over onto a patch of desert. Al immediately gets out. He's pissed (he doesn't like surprises), but is reluctantly ready for anything. The wind picks up, and Al squints to see through a dustsheet of small desert particles as he stoically scans the topography. In the car, Peabody fiddles with the device, occasionally look-

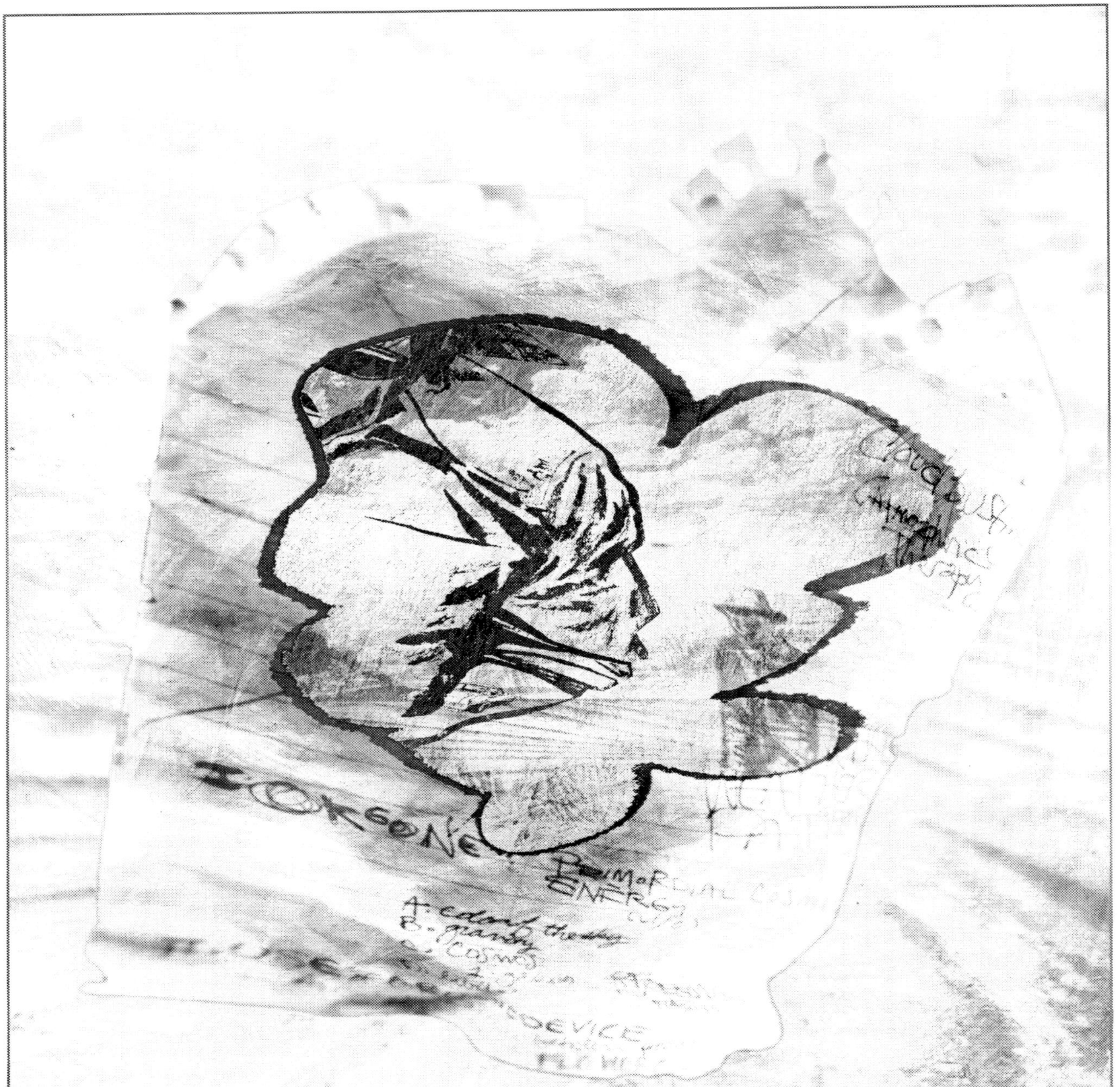

malloy '05

looking up to see what's happening as Al walks out into the desert and is gone for a good half hour. Eventually, night falls.

Al makes it back. Whew! He's an ominous site. He cups his black derby with his bony hand as his rail thin frame slices through the windy sheets of sand. He gets in, and Peabody anxiously asks, "What was it? Was it a new intelligence?" "Yes, and a relatively harmless one," Al says, "but they are screwing with us. I think the word's out. There are more coming." Al motions for Peabody to go back the opposite way. Peabody swings the Buick around and bolts back in the other direction as they begin looking for signs of orgonomy (unusual botanical activity) which inadvertently emanates around the *Ea*[1], this is one way they are tipped off. Peabody gets nervous and whispers, "I can't stand being late. I hate that, it's like were wasting our time if we're even just a little late, seconds to late and run the risk that the hole wont fill properly." "Cool your pistons soldier!" snorts Al. They can see a flickering orange light off to the West that's oscillating back and forth very rapidly. They veer off the highway immediately, and after a couple miles the Buick speeds past a rusty sign that reads:

B L M

NO TRESSPASSING
USE OF DEADLY FORCE IS AUTHORIZED
VIOLATORS WILL BE PROSECUTED TO
THE FULL EXTENT OF THE LAW
BUREAU OF LAND MANAGEMENT

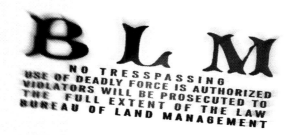

They lock onto a fine, green mist swirling around off in the distance and barrel straight for it. Al's senses go into hyper-drive. "OVER THERE FREEMAN!" he shouts, as they begin to hone in on the target. Peabody veers to the right. "Up there, a little closer, getting closer... closer... CLOSER!" Al shouts, "STOP THE CAR!" He remains sternly focused as he gets out of the Buick with a dramatic, rapid gait. His run could be mistaken for skipping as he progresses several yards, then stops and starts, stops and starts. "Right... right... RIGHT HERE!" he shouts, stopping at what appears to be an ordinary desert mound. Peabody is bobbling along closely behind with his duffle bag. Al yells, "RIGHT HERE NOW!" and then FAWOOOOSHHHHH!!! The glowing, undulating orb fires out of the earth like an atomic cannon, arching with neon red, orange, and white plasma. It's a fascinating sight! This time it seemed to linger in view for a lot longer than usual before disappearing into the upper atmosphere. Peabody pounces down on the lip of the hole and hurriedly configures the device based on what he sees, and to think, only a few months ago he still needed to mark the hole to make sure he knew where it was. He triggers the device... and nothing happens. His face goes ghost white as he nervously reconfigures the device. Beads of sweat begin to trickle down his face, even though it's the moon, not the sun, beating down on him. Before he can take another stab at it, nineteen and a half grueling seconds go by, he fires the device again and the hole finally fills itself, rather un-dramatically , "Ploopff!" Putting the device back in the duffle bag, he says without question, "Al... it's getting bigger... it's definitely... getting bigger." "Yeah...I know," says Al, "I know."

1. EA: E [*energy*] A [*alpha* or primodial] Also an acronym for *Enigma*.

chapter eight

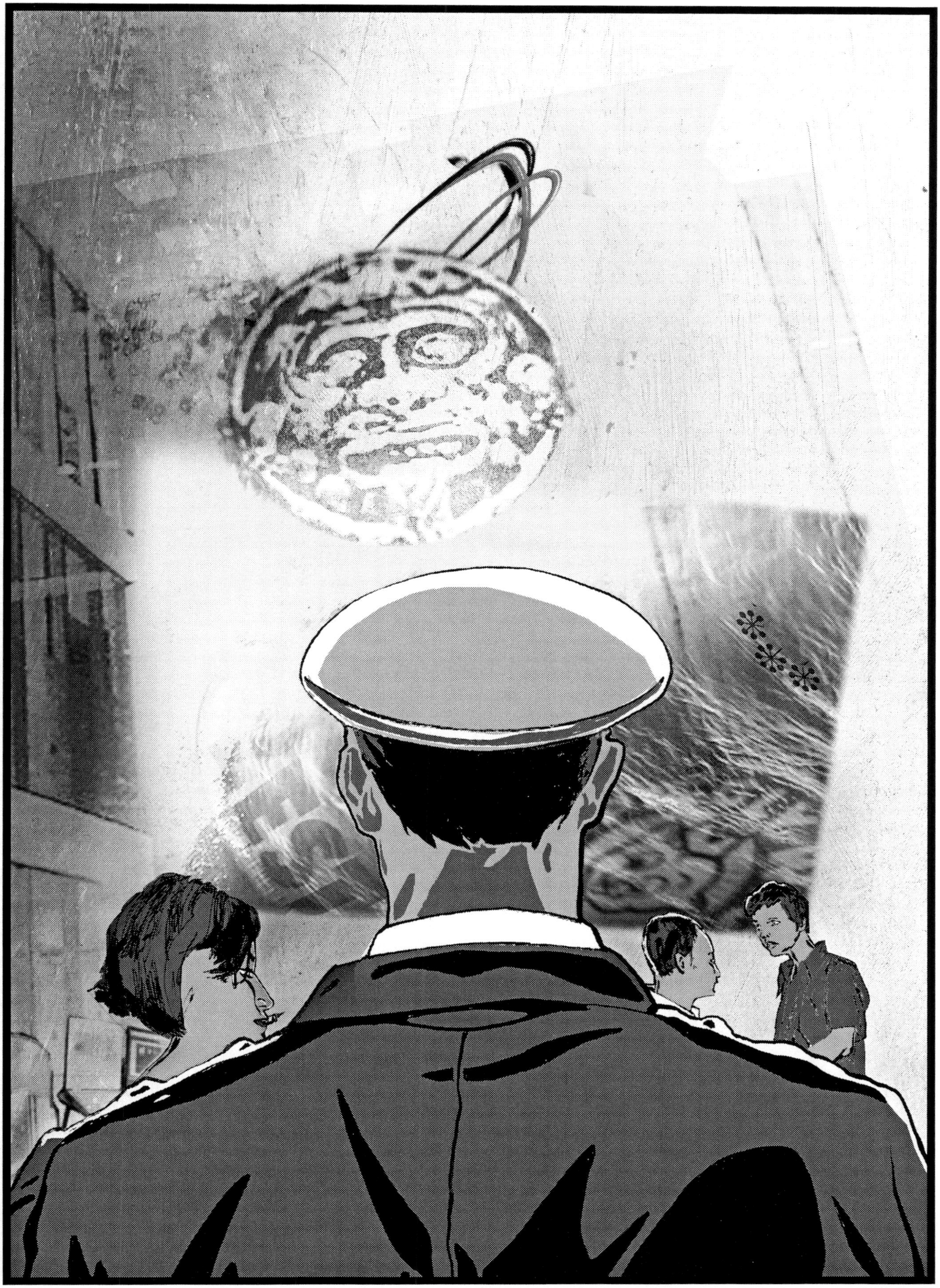

MALLOY '05

It's only after much practice that Browning is able to project himself far enough out-side his body to get the attention of the Shaman. He's almost severed his astral cord a few times, but is by far the most gifted in this area, at least as far as the RV program knows. He's more like an athlete than a mystic, always working to perform better for longer periods of time. He trains just like an astronaut would, constantly rehearsing and reviewing his steps to achieve contact and do his part. Browning knows the government's already accept-ed that chaos[1] is in full swing and that it's no longer a matter of if, but when and where the can will tip. He puts on his best poker face as he walks into the briefing room with Colonel Ramsey and the Professor, who's wearing his military uniform, upon which there is a gold ID bar stamped: Lt. Col. Stockwell. The room is large and cold. Its remote corners are crammed with desks and computer screens and stacks upon stacks of papers. On the wall is a large circular sculpture with a grimacing deity in the center, directly across from the sculpture is an atomic clock that reads 09:05:14. They are joined by several quasi-fashion-able, hipster type men and women in their mid-twenties to early thirties. Ramsey immedi-ately asks, "Where's the board?" The head hipster with a large piercing in his left eyebrow reports, "They couldn't be here. We are going to have to video-conference to all active loca-tions. When we get directives, the team here will handle all the dissemination." This is disturbing news for the Lieutenant Colonel. They now sit in silence as a robotic voice timer counts backwards from 10 seconds: 5,4,3,2,1... When a beep emits from the satel-lite conference phone, Lieutenant Colonel Stockwell speaks:

I. Chaos: The confused, unorganized condition of mass or matter before the creation of distinct and orderly forms.

"Gentleman, as you know, Special Assignments Operative Browning was successful in arranging a rendezvous with our source. Colonel Ramsey and myself were there to witness the exchange of information, and later have it analyzed by the Montauk Committee. We have this to report:

The wave of novelty that has advanced unbroken since the birth of our solar system has now fully focused and terminally coalesced itself in our species. Time consciousness is now accelerating at an alarming rate. We have only been able to engage in damage control from the innumerable side effects in an attempt to hold back the further acceleration of perceived time. All foundations and structures will inevitably cease as technology becomes nanotechnology and we dissipate from our physical presence. This will happen soon. The novelty wave demands an unachievable and infinite level of creativity to sustain this hyper-reality. Technology has reached an apex and has morphed into pure redundancy, fed by the limitations of the human container. This escalation can best be described as an uncontrollable virus with no cure. We cannot predict or understand the totality of the outcome. It has been made clear that the planet has been stretched to its finite limits. What comes after the event will be a world that we cannot directly control."

There are less than 9 days prior to 2012.

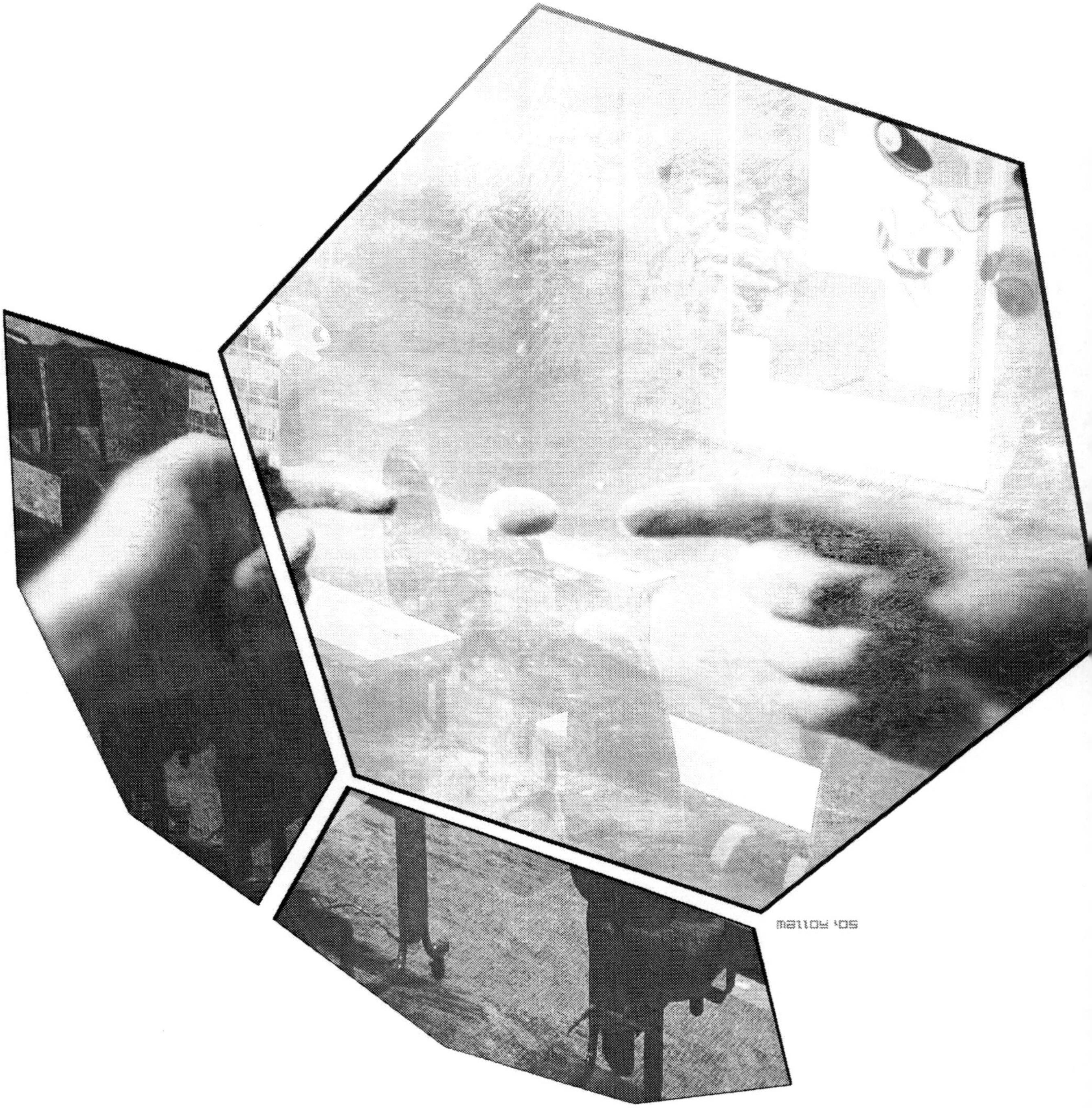
malloy '05

Alone in the training room Browning uses the simulator to try and push himself further. He still has many questions of his own. All personnel have left to be with their families and loved ones. But because Browning is a Montauk Baby, he really doesn't have a family per se, even though he was adopted out after the project was closed down.

chapter nine

He was stunted from the beginning as many were, but ironically it was natural for him to end up in the Army. In some cases, the military is the only real option for many such young men with no other way to escape an otherwise bleak existence. Many became bag-boys, clerks, or shoe-shiners in small towns across the country. That's how they normally relocated "the babies". Without supervision, Browning feels paranoid because the train-ing room is strictly business. Usually there's an agenda, or a task that gets handed down. They perform the task and that's it - nothing more, nothing less, strictly military busi-ness, period. Many times, Browning has encountered ethereal shapes and seen alarm-ingly bizarre and colorful little people, who laugh and carry bits of spinning light. He's attempted to go the extra mile and share these experiences with the directive commander who always tells him to simply disregard them, as to not lose focus on the astral missions at hand. Nothing else really matters to Browning other than understanding what he's seen. He journey's deeper into his trance meditation and finally feels his head resonate with the *music of the spheres*[1]. Without warning, they arrive. He is surrounded by elf-like entities as his vision becomes blurry and everything buzzes. Fear takes hold. He thinks they are laughing at him as he feels himself slipping into a parallel realm. But he fights the fear as he heads deeper into the caverns of his mind. He has to know why, he must know why. He knows he cannot suppress the empty void that so many have avoided by assuming the role of brainwashed consumer/religion puppets. He feels lost and alone in the outside world. He's never known safety or even love really. There is an imminent sense of finality to Browning's quest, driven by something he doesn't yet understand.

I. MUSIC OF THE SPHERES: a. An inaudible music that Pythagoras thought was produced by celestial beings. b. An ancient doctrine originating with the Greeks that implies that the universe and everything in it is in harmony.

On the drive back to the Motel6, Peabody and Al are a little more frayed than usual. Peabody's concern is that they haven't heard anything from home base in over a week. This has never happened. Home base is ALWAYS concerned with their progress. Al suddenly erupts "What the hell do they care? Treating us like underground fugitives! They don't know WHAT they're doing and never HAVE! It's just one debacle after another since '38!"

After his eruption, he sits calmly and stares out the window for a couple of tense moments, then says at a considerably lesser volume, "Look, you're right. All we can do is focus on our part and hope for the best. There is just no way to predict the outcome. We've got to factor in all possible aspects of Chaos that may come into play in our favor." Peabody bites his lower lip as he often does when enduring Al's tirade's, which often morph into monologues. Peabody is now bobbing his head back and forth like he's reading the Torah. Always running figures in the back of his mind, Peabody has never given up looking for a way to contain the horror he's largely responsible for unleashing. His burden is heavy and Al knows this, but for the most part can't help his disgust not just for Peabody, but for all of humanity. Al re-remembers one of his former lives, when he lived on a farm with a wife and child. Everyday, he would get up to feed the livestock and routinely embark on the long list of chores.

The family worked and existed together in total harmony. They were completely content. He doesn't recall a TV, only a radio around which they would gather to listen to in the evenings. Even though he's not sure if it really happened or not or if he was really even there, he is sure that the human race began its final descent around this period. He has total contempt for the prototypical trend-following automatons that define the current population. "Hell in a hand basket!" he often thinks to himself. "They should all be in baby diapers with lollipops to suck on all day!" he snorts, appalled that the White Diapered Kids, as he affectionately calls them, are procreating at all let alone in advancing numbers. They themselves being spoiled, ignorant children in his eyes.

As the sun comes down over the desert on yet another grueling day, Al can't help himself as he sarcastically rants "While the world continues on with its daily routine, its societies scurrying about frantically, completely locked into systems and behaviors that cannot be sustained, living like blind moles in an ever deepening ignorance all while time on earth is running short, Peabody and Al, the dynamic duo somehow find the strength to go on!" Exhaustedly, Al throws the tape recorder back on the dash. Peabody responds with a painful grimace. He is accustomed to Al's banter and understands that Al has lost everything, including things he never really had but re-remembers and holds dear. Deep down, Al is holding on to a thread, to the slightest chance that this all might stop. There's a distant possibility that he could assume a normal, yet simple existence with some stability and maybe even a female companion.

Peabody would do anything to make this happen, if in some way he could make this possible for Al, who's suffered so much, it would relieve him of at least some of the guilt. If they abandon accident duty, there is no replacing them. It would mean they are throwing in the towel on the planet and its future. They know it's critical to plug the holes, otherwise the Ea wouldn't be so interested in assisting them. All they can do is continue... and cling to their individual dreams.

chapter ten

On the morning of December 31st, 2011, Al and Peabody are arguing with the Motel6 manager because their Chemical Bank credit card is maxed out. They know this has never happened before. They also know that the credit card is how HQ keeps tabs on them, making the situation even more disconcerting. After years on the road and many lonely Christmas holidays together it comes down to this: bickering about a measly hotel bill, while "accidents" are occurring quite possibly inches from where Bob, the Motel6 manager, is currently standing. The absurdity of this, in light of the fact that they might be the only ones holding it together for all of humanity, is surreal to say the least. They know they need to get out into the field, and that another accident is always on its way. If only there was a way to stop it, to destroy it once and for all.

DING! The sound of the elevator causes a momentary reprieve as Barbara Wexler emerges. She's a mature, professional executive dressed sensibly with a gold jacket and slacks, who could easily be confused with a Century 21 realtor. Not only is she a successful business woman, but she moonlights as a prominent paranormal researcher as well. She's considered the Barbara Walters of the field for that matter.

She immediately recognizes Peabody (who's pretty hard to miss), and says "Mr. Freeman! – Oh.... and... Mr. Leedskalnin! What a pleasure! I'm here for UFOCON 2012, are you attending?" "NAWW!" Al snorts, "You of all people should know we don't do those things Miss Wexler, I presume?" "Yes, yes, that's right," she replies. "Well, Ms. Wexler, my associate and I are very busy saving the mundane from extinction and our employer has seen fit to not be available to settle our hotel accommodations. We don't carry cash as its against our principles but we'll gladly accept your relentless requests for an interview if you will assist us. You see, we have something extremely important to attend to as we speak," says Al. Peabody turns sharply to Al and glares at him, alarmed by this proposal. "I would be honored to assist you Mr. Leedskalnin!" Barbara says. She's almost euphoric at the opportunity.. "Thank you kindly, Ms. Wexler. If you like, we can meet here tomorrow, same time?" "Excellent," she says, "And thank you SO much for this opportunity. There are so many who are interested in what you have to say." "AWWW, HOGWASH!" barks Al, who's overcome with a hint of celebrity, "But if it makes you happy, I'll do it." He nods and gives her a wink. "Thank you again, Mr. Leedskalnin," says Barbara. "Call me Al", he says, "For chrissakes.. please. Now, if you'll excuse us we've got some things to attend to," grunts Peabody. "Most certainly," she says, sauntering to the checkout counter, giving her credit card to Bob, the Motel6 manager. "I'll handle that."

Back on the desert highway, Peabody looks over at Al, scowling at him. Al ignores the glaring stare and mutters, "I can feel atmospheric pressure pulling from the southeast. We need to get on the 375." Peabody acknowledges this, then goes back to scowling at Al, finally saying, "What the hell are you thinking Al?! An interview with Barbara Wexler? Ohhh, that's a GREEEAAT idea. Why didn't I think of that?! I can't wait for the black helicopters to pick us up and dump us in a

malloy '05

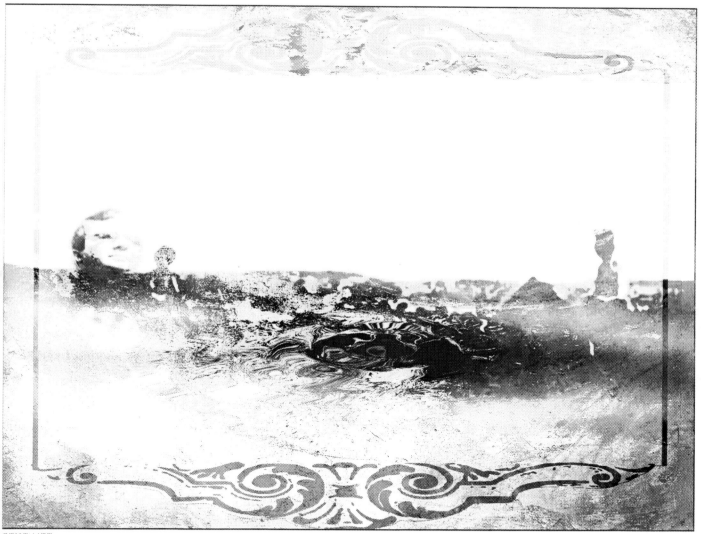

desert cavern so the vultures can peck at us until we die!" "C'MON KID! The jig is up. It's over!" snaps Al. "That coincidence back there was the supreme collective subconscious at full throttle, or, maybe the *greys*[1] are at it again. Either way, it doesn't matter. It's obvious we're on our own now. HQ has been abandoned, WE'VE BEEN ABANDONED! It's every man for himself Freeman! We're on our own. I've got a feeling that tomorrow will bring some answers to all this madness, so why not? Why not give the people something to really chew on, spill the beans a little? I'll bet you that after a couple days, if we're all still around, they'll forget all about it anyway, like a herd of cows The last thing they'll want to do is wake from their brainwashed stupors. Right now we've got a hole to fill Freeman!. It's SOP, FREEMAN, *SOP*[2]!!!"

Sometimes they get a break. After only 15 miles, Peabody's glasses start accumulating condensation as they continue to barrel up the 375. They can see some cloud clusters over a rolling plain in the distance. Peabody turns onto the 421 and they charge on toward a large, remote cattle ranch. As they edge out onto the open fields, a few ranchers on horseback see them from across the plain. Al jumps out, scurries to open the gate and grumbles, "Don't want to bust down the gate and have them Cowboys shooting at us again goddammit! Let's do this thing, Freeman!" Peabody floors the Buick as they race toward the yet undetermined exact location while hot on their tails are the Cowboys, the kind who don't go into town much and are probably bored to tears. They come racing after them, hooping and hollering on their ranch steeds. The thundering hoof beats get louder and louder. Peabody and Al's hearts are racing as they drive over cowpies and potholes in the pasture as Al feverishly hones in on the accident. After a few seconds, he exclaims, "STOP! HURRY! STOP!" Peabody floors the brakes as dirt and grass fly everywhere. "HURRY!" Al screams, "IT'S GOING TO BE BIG! I CAN SEE IT IN MY HEAD!" Al runs looking straight ahead and abruptly slides/stops over a pile of cow dung. "HERE!" he stammers, "IT'S BIG, FREEMAN!" Between the dozen cowboys racing after them and Peabody and Al's scurrying, the scene is cacophonous. Then, in the very next instant:

FAWOOOOOOOOOO

1. GREY: The most commonly reported alien being. Rather small and humanoid, it has big, black, almond-shaped eyes, and measures on average 1.0m - 1.25m in height.
2. SOP: Standard Operating Procedure. A term made popular in the Armed Forces in the 1930's.

OSSSSSSSHHHHHHHHHHHHHHHHHHHHHHHH!!!

Like a meteor fired out of a slingshot, a **HUGE** arching ball of orange light, crackling with 6-foot white and blue sparks shooting off in all directions, rockets out of the earth. It looks like a morphing atomic reaction.

Ascending out of sight after what feels like minutes, the moment after can only be described as profoundly quiet. There is no noise... not one sound, not a peep from anyone. All mouths are agape, including Peabody's, when Al screams, "FREEMAN! HOLE!!!" Peabody looks down, his eyes ogle and nearly pop out of his head in horror as he sees a 20 foot wide hole with debris trickling back in and vaporous gases from the energy involved spewing outward from some of the crevices. Peabody snaps to and places the device on the edge of the heaving hole, setting the potentiometer all the way to the right for the first time. He fires it, nothing happens. He tries it again... nothing happens. Al becomes noticeably frightened. He ponders the immensity of what this means, that the earth itself will be mortally compromised if this is allowed to continue, that the planet will soon be pulled apart by *angular momentum*[1]. As Peabody sits staring at the hole on the verge of a final nervous breakdown, the ranchers are trying to steady their horses and are too dumbfounded to speak. Suddenly the ground begins to shake. The horses whinny and snort as an undulating wave moves across the prairie with 5 foot ripples finally terminating at the hole, which collapses in on itself with the sound of an imploding dirt pocket "KERPLOOOF!" The final gasp of the event.

Al and Peabody look at each other in utter astonishment for a moment before they begin to scurry straight back to the Buick, utilizing their pavlovian instinct. The ranchers don't move at all. They are still trying to wrap their brains around what they've just witnessed, when from beyond the mountain ridge, the first enormous UFO appears...

I. ANGULAR MOMENTUM: Obtained by multiplying the mass of an orbiting body by its velocity and the radius of its orbit. According to the conservation laws of physics,the angular momentum of any orbiting body must remain constant at all points in the orbit [i.e. it cannot be created or destroyed, only altered]. If the orbit is elliptical the radius will vary. Since the mass is constant, the velocity changes. An example of this are the planets in our solar system.

chapter eleven

Peabody is mumbling, "Is it happening? Is it real? Are... are they probing us?" Al is also in a sort of daze, but reacts comfortably to the situation as if he's used to it. It would seem that he's conscious but cannot move. He and the others are paralyzed and aren't able to lift so much as a pinkie. Peabody continues to stare forward, whispering "Is this really real... is that a ufo?"

The Ea emerge from the moist ether. They begin to gather around the Buick and the cattle ranchers, as if inspecting them somewhat curiously. The taller ones gather around the hole. They turn their elliptical heads toward it with a concerned nod. They're aware it has been allowed to get too big. Even though it's against the cosmic order of cause and effect, they now must assess the damage and freeze the immediate surroundings in order to do so. They have no choice. The time has come for them to intervene. The Ea are a sight to be felt. They're more like thin fuzzy forms than the grey aliens that were co-manufactured with the military in the late 30's, way before the first wave of sightings in '47. The instructions to grow and assemble them is what led to the Montauk Babies program. Even the Ea are alarmed by the greys.

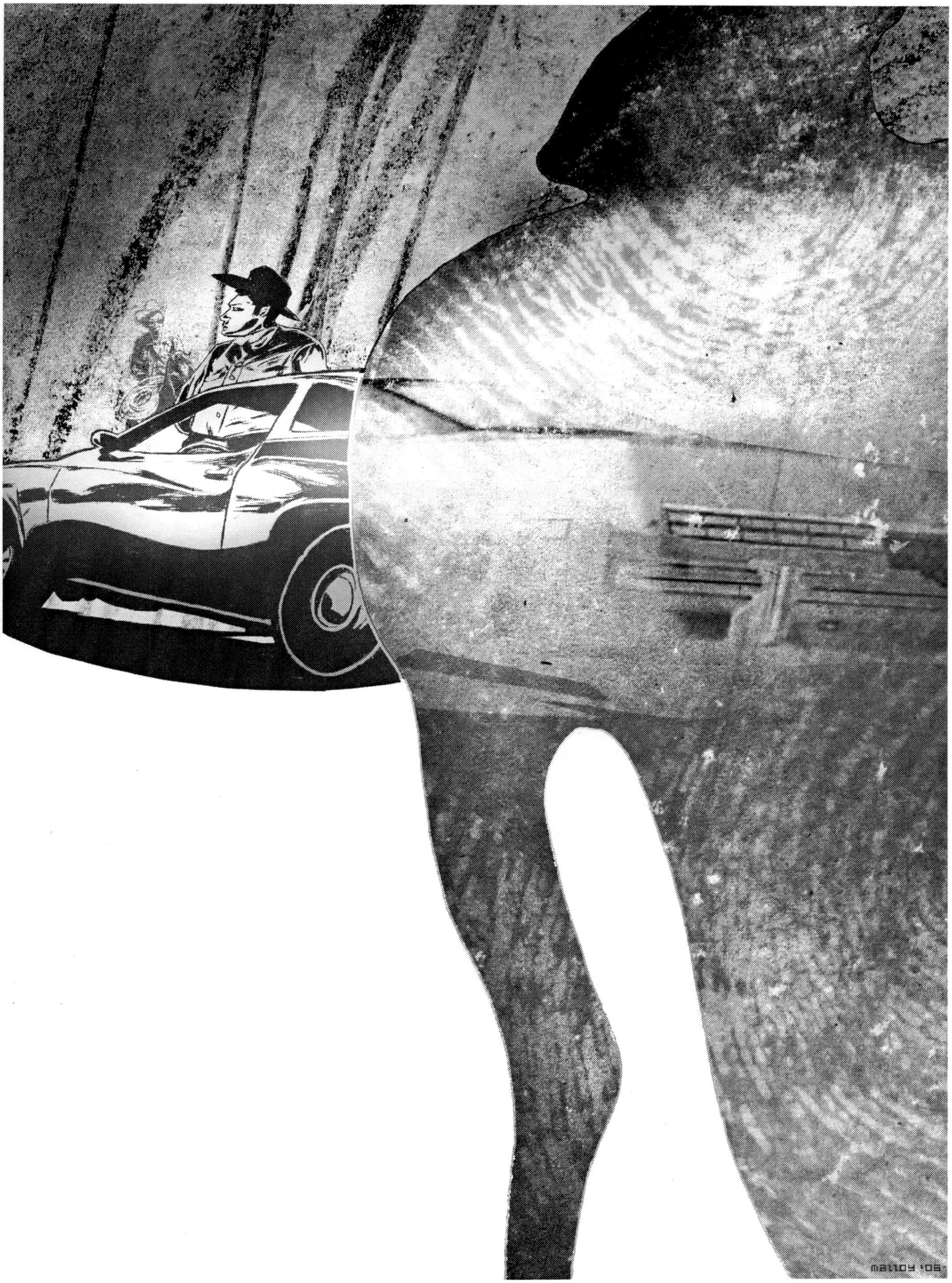
malloy '06

The tallest of the three just floats by the hole for what seems like hours, but are more than likely nano-seconds. Being face to face with the magnificence of the Ea is like conquering your fear of the boogie man by standing in front of him and confronting every crevice in his hideous, horrifying face. On a scale of 1 to 10, their presence is off the map. In fact, there is no map. They are so magnificent that it is impossible not to be in total awe. Humans don't have a choice in the matter. They are more or less rendered useless before them. The Ea don't need to impose any sort of mind control, because the humans basically do it to themselves. The crippling gnosis that humans experience is a self imposed reaction to the unknown, through the crude filters of the six senses (the Vatican knows this as do the Tibetan monks and every powerful world religion for that matter). Even though the Ea exist in parallel with the Earth plane, they oscillate in a different dimension altogether. They reside in the 7th and most elusive state, which is hyper-consciousness.

After only a few more moments, the Ea, and all that appeared with them, slowly dissipates and then simply vanishes. Al regains full control while Peabody and the others are still squirming out of their stupor. There is a dim silence over the ranchers who look like they all have severe Budweiser hangovers. With mouths agape, they just watch Al and Peabody get back into the Buick. Peabody puts the vehicle in gear and slowly meanders toward the gate, squishing through a few piles of cow manure on the way. At the gate, he does a couple of mini burnouts as he groggily comes completely to his senses. He hits his head on the steering wheel a couple times and finally recovers his ability to drive.

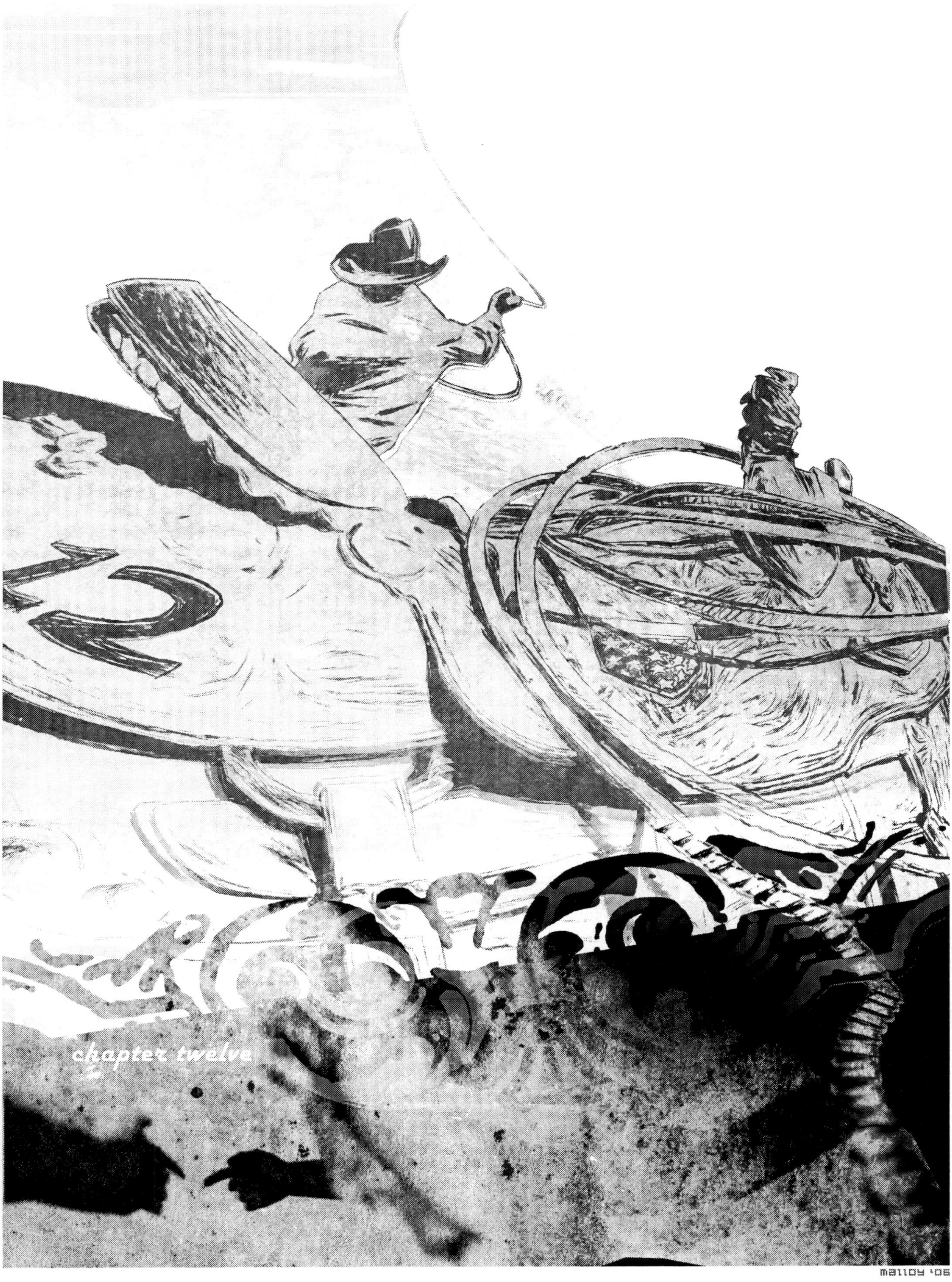
chapter twelve
malloy '06

Back in the training room, Browning's astral cord snaps him back into his body. When he comes to his senses, he is sweating and panting trying to catch his breath. He is in the Crypto-Labs at the training base, all alone. He has a distant yet familiar link to Al even though they have never met, he is somehow compelled towards Al's energy field when astral traveling, or employing **MAX RV**. It's a strong pull that enabled Browning to clearly witness the event on the cattle ranch with the Ea. Because he was disembodied and wasn't physically there, he had the opportunity to observe and retain what he witnessed, proving to himself what he already knew. There *are* invisible worlds, and the militaries and governments of the world have known this for thousands of years. It's not so much the fact that there are aliens and endless life forms throughout the cosmos, that's beside the point. It's the fact that the earth is replete with manmade distractions designed to perpetually exclude this realization from the masses, and gloss over the fact that the earth is in serious trouble.

It suddenly dawns on Browning that all humans have the capacity to leave their bodies at will... anytime they desire. He thinks to himself that it must have been this way once, long, long ago. He thinks to himself - surely, the *Nazca Lines*[1] and the great pyramids were seen by the most ancient gods as they flew, disembodied, over the landscapes from Africa to Babylonia. His interest in these places was initially peaked when he was ordered to fight for his country in the original Gulf War. Even though he was labeled a rowdy metal head, in his spare time he would seek to learn more about these strange lands. He remembers hearing from Boaz, the impoverished Egyptian priest he befriended, telling him that select initiates, such as the Pharaohs, were brought forth into the light and could emulate these Gods by astral travel in another dimension. Browning now understands this to be the dimension of the Ea. He realizes that if this door were to be revealed, if the tools to open this box were laid in front of mankind, then there would be no way to rule or control. Perhaps this is the way things were long, long ago...100,000, 200,000 years or more before Christ. There would be no secrets, there would be no rules, there would be no laws and lastly there would be no reason for much of anything that man has been responsible for since the time of Egypt. Browning knows now that he's nothing more than an abomination. He is the Zeitgeist , the seer who sees behind the veil and whose purpose is to be a translator for the people who are in many ways very similar to himself. He realizes that the Shaman is really a voice for the *Elementals*[2], who cannot be directly perceived. They already know the end and how it will happen. As old as the earth itself, the Elementals are eternally ready to reveal all to any that can see them in the higher astral realms. They have provided direction in the distant past, back when man listened. They would manifest as wolves, cats, birds, and at times, even humans, just as one was doing now, via the Shaman. Browning is greatly relieved and can now see things clearly for the very first time.

I. NAZCA LINES: Geoglyphs located on a high, arid plateau in the Peruvian desert that stretches for 37 miles between the towns of Nazca and Palpa. The lines form drawings including a hummingbird, monkey, spider, and a massive, human-like figure resembling a modern-day astronaut. The lines were created between 200 B.C. and 600 A.D., but could be thousands of years older.

2. ELEMENTALS: Ethereal beings that represent the four elements of creation [earth, air, fire, and water]. They are considered to be supernatural beings composed of pure energy. These sometimes mischievous spirits, never human to begin with, have existed long before mankind's arrival. They dwell mainly in natural locations, such as forests, fields, lakes, rivers, volcanoes, deserts, etc.,; and places considered sacred.

"You gentlemen are paid-up through the first, here are your new cards," says Bob, the Motel6 manager, "Courtesy of Ms. Wexler." Al gives Bob a cold stare, and an equally fatigued Peabody grabs the room cards whilst scooping a handful of candies from the hospitality tray. Heading back to the room, as they walk toward the elevators, Al hears the sounds return inside his head, "GRKKKKKK...GRKKKKKKKK...kkk..." He is too tired to be scared that he might fall apart or demolecularize at this very moment. He just needs to lay down and rest. In Al's room, Peabody prepares the device while Al lays back perfectly straight and motionless on the bed. You could say Al has lived at least a half dozen too many lives. Once again, Peabody gently lowers the device as it emits a low hum into Al's chest.

"Eermmm   ergghh..."   mumbles   Al.

chapter

thirteen

"Yes... yes. I'll be there. Mmm... yes Ms. Wexler, of course. Mmm.. Ms.Wexler - ummmmghh." Al is very groggy after last night's repair session with Peabody. An anxious Ms. Wexler has called his room at 9:33 AM, and asked Al if they can do the UFOCON 2012 interview at 11 o'clock. Al probably doesn't even realize this until Peabody comes pounding on the door. "Al?" he yells, "What's going on in there? Al? Let me in." With the skin tone and grimace of an auto wreck survivor, Al gets up fully clothed and lets Peabody in. He immediately gets horizontal again, putting the back of his hand over his eyes as if to shield him from the sun. Peabody occupies half the room nervously, and says, "I got a phone call from a Damon.. Al... Al? Did you agree to do the interview AT the UFOCON? Al?!" It's been a brutal ride the last several years for both of them, but somehow today feels different. Al mutters "yeah... yeah... I guess I did kid. Someone's got to get it down. I figure it's time. We've been at this for too long. We need to let those idiots know the truth. The jig is up Freeman! THE JIG IS FUCK-ING UP!" Peabody just stares at Al while sitting down on the edge of the small Motel6 bed, causing it to arch somewhat with Al bowing upwards like a cross bow. He doesn't know what to say. He looks at Al, then reaches for his pocket protector, nervously checking all the gadgets that he needs at his disposal. Somehow Al finds the will to get up and says, "C'mon Freeman! What the hell! Lets give them their money's worth."

Down in the lobby, Barbara Wexler and her small entourage are ready to escort Al and Peabody down to the UFOCON, a few blocks away at the convention center. Al has his full sun-blocking wraparound glasses on and makes a beeline through the busy lobby area, through the sliding door of the blue shuttle van with Peabody directly in tow, desperately trying to stuff himself into the front passenger seat. Ms. Wexler closes the sliding door from inside and says, "Well, it's great to finally have this opportunity with you." Al himself looks like an alien with the wraparounds on. He can be hard to warm up to especially in the morning. "Yeah..." he says, "Really great... say... will you and your friends be whooping it up tonight? Being it's New Year's eve and all." He is prod-ding as he usually does in any social situation and being a Montauk Baby, he lacks familiarity with certain graces and can be misperceived as cynical. "Oh no, nothing like that," she says, "we'll probably have a late dinner and spend the evening together. There will be film crews and even some news reporters to document the day's events. We did make sure we had some champagne though. Would you and Mr. Freeman like to spend New Year's Eve with us?" nervously Peabody shakes his head in the front seat at the mention of film and news crews, fumbling with his pocket protector. Al notices this and says, "I don't think that will be possible Ms. Wexler. But thanks all the same."

After a moment of awkward silence, Barbara proceeds to tell Al about a recent cattle mutilation, where she and her team discovered "alien" tools and instruments. Apparently, the pieces were left behind in haste and the most stringent of scientific committees have indeed deter-mined that the materials are of unearthly origin, due to their mineral composition. Al hacks and giggles and says, "My dear Ms. Wexler, I can appreciate your tenacity but I suggest you look into the world of the small, the infinitesimally small that is.... to find the answers that you seek." "Why, what do you mean?" inquiries Ms. Wexler. "I mean there was no reason to go to the moon or any other planet for that matter because it all starts and stops right here," he exclaims, pointing to his cranium. As the shuttle van pulls up to the convention center, there is a huge bug-eyed grey alien balloon on the rooftop of the main entrance. It would be impossible to miss and certainly doesn't help the legitimacy of the event. Al heaves a heavy sigh upon beholding it as he gets out of the vehicle.

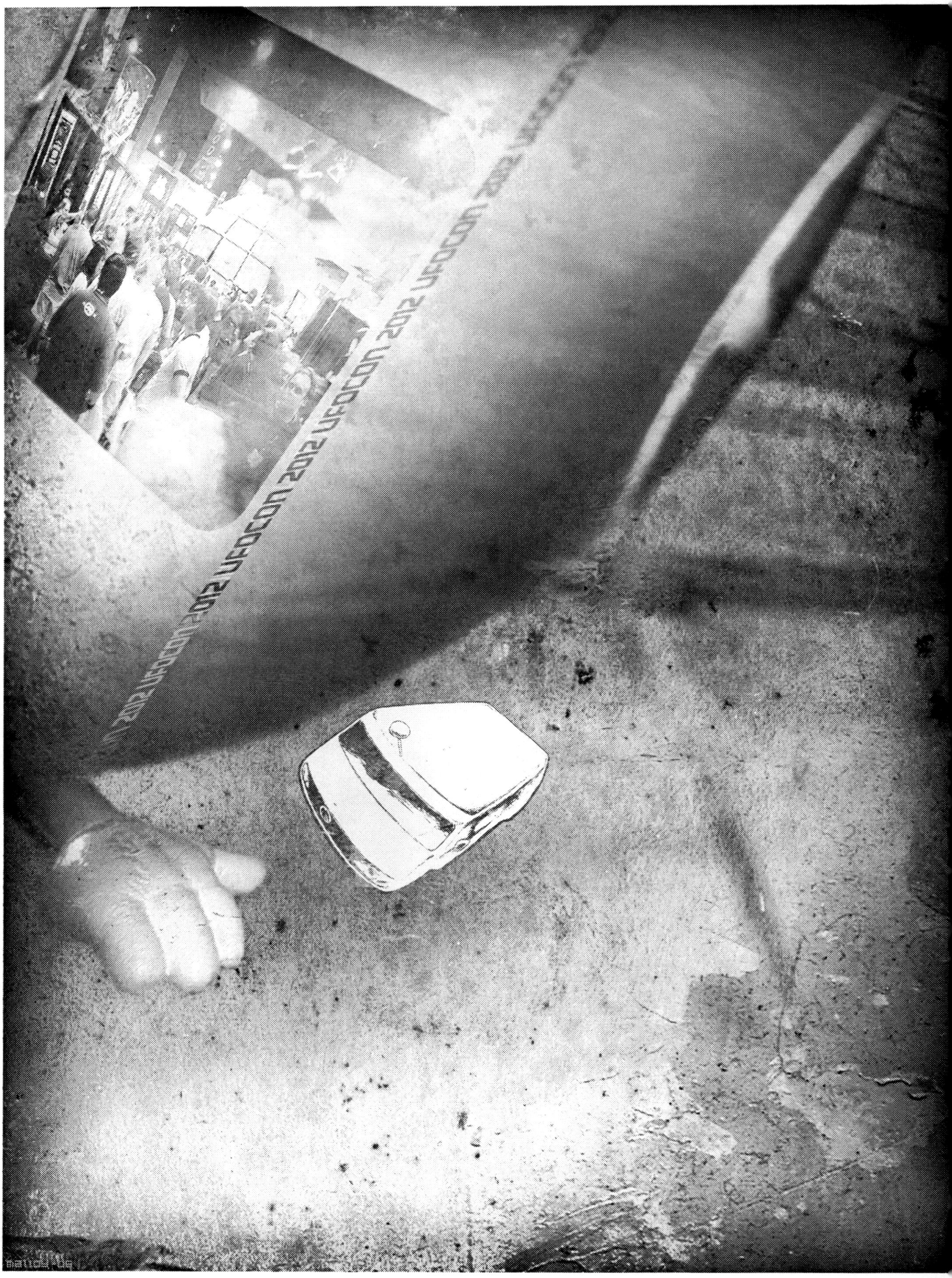
2012 UFOCON 2012 UFOCON 2012 UFOCON 2012 UFOCON 2012 UFOCON

As they enter the large convention center lobby, en route to the green room, Peabody notices that there are two looming figures in the food court off to the side and in front of the Subway. He can see that the smaller one, who looks a lot like Al, is peering at him from behind a large plastic indoor plant. They are awkward and alarming visages. Even the people standing in line for the half sandwich special are staring at them. "Right this way", says Damon, Ms. Wexler's assistant, "we've got some beverages and food items for you while we prepare the auditorium." Just then, Peabody snaps AUDITORIUM? What AUDITORIUM? ... Al?" Barbara interjects, "Why yes, we discussed that this morning Mr. Leedskalnin. You do recall, don't you?" After a tense pause, Al responds in a more grizzled than normal voice, "Ms. Wexler, I only know how to re-remember I'm afraid. But if I did agree... then I did. So, how many people do you figure will be present?" A relieved Barbara admits, "Oh, I would say a thousand or so." "Fabulous!" says Al, "Just fabulous." Peabody grabs several hors d'oeuvre's at the hospitality able and nervously shakes his head, double-checking his pocket protector.

As Ms. Wexler and Damon go about the affair, Peabody slips off and goes back down the hall and peers out into the volume of conventioneers. He looks above and past the crowd to see if he can repeat his sighting of the two figures, which he does. He sees them in the Cortez ballroom where endless authors and UFO carnies sell their wares. They are bumping into each other, trying to escape the Psychotronics booth, which is furious with activity as a young man levitates in a luminescent, orb-like structure. A sign above the machine reads: The Orbitron. As Peabody follows the two figures, he realizes there's something awkward and not quite right about their movements. The tall one keeps bumping into conventioneers, trying to disguise himself by holding a large cotton candy cone in front of his face. Peabody scurries down the hall back to the greenroom, where Ms. Wexler is sitting next to Al, discussing the interview. After a polite forced smile from Peabody, Ms. Wexler gets up to continue her preparations. Peabody sits down on the couch, his 350 plus pounds bringing Al even closer to him and urgently whispers, "The clones are back, Al. The clones... their back." Al doesn't even blink. He had really forgotten all about the clones. He knows that they are real, and that he's not just re-remembering, because of the scars on his back from the last skirmish. "Grrrrrkk... Grrkrrrrrrrrrrkk," Al glitches, but shakes it off, "Gggggrkkkkk." "We're ready for you now Mr. Leedskalnin," says Damon. "If you'll come with me please." Al looks like a deer lost in the headlights as Damon helps him get off the sofa. With Peabody right alongside him, they head down the hallway to the stage entry ramp. Just then, Damon says to Peabody, "You can watch from here. We've got a special area set aside for you." "Oh, gee... thanks!" says Peabody. Al quips, "It'll be alright Freeman. Cool your pistons."

chapter fourteen

Up on the platform there are two chairs. It's a modular set with low lighting in an intimate setting, reminiscent of the Dick Cavett Show of the '60's (before intelligent programming was ultimately deemed non-marketable). From stage right emerges Ms. Wexler. She is the essence of credibility in the field of the paranormal, exhibiting a certain grace and regality that directly commands one's respect. She walks to the center of the stage and begins to address the crowd through a small wireless lavaliere microphone pinned to her lapel. Damon is stage right, and is attaching a similar microphone to Al's moderately worn, black suit. Al stares straight ahead.

Wexler begins, "It is truly astounding that we have this opportunity today. After almost a century of denial from our world governments regarding their experiments in space and time travel, as well as the use of human beings, moreover American human beings as cattle... as nothing more than organic matter devoid of soul. The timeline isn't clear, but we know that something of immense proportions happened in the mid 1940's. We now know that Einstein, Tesla, and countless others ultimately refused to be involved in what we believe has developed into the number one concern for our military forces around the globe. We've obtained startling information from the recent discovery of Tesla's final diary which was removed by the FBI upon his death from his apartment in New York. This information confirms that he was indeed communicating with an alien intelligence. Among the data, complex mathematical formulas were found that are currently being analyzed by our greatest scientific minds, but we have yet to decode the significance of these findings. We have yet to find the key to this *Rosetta Stone*[1] of unknown magnitude."

2. ROSETTA STONE: Discovered in Egypt in 1799 by Napoleon Bonaparte, a section of an inscribed granite slate that was originally about 6 feet tall and dated back to 196 B.C. It's inscriptions in heiroglyphics, Demotic, and Greek gave the first clues to deciphering Egyprian heiroglyphics.

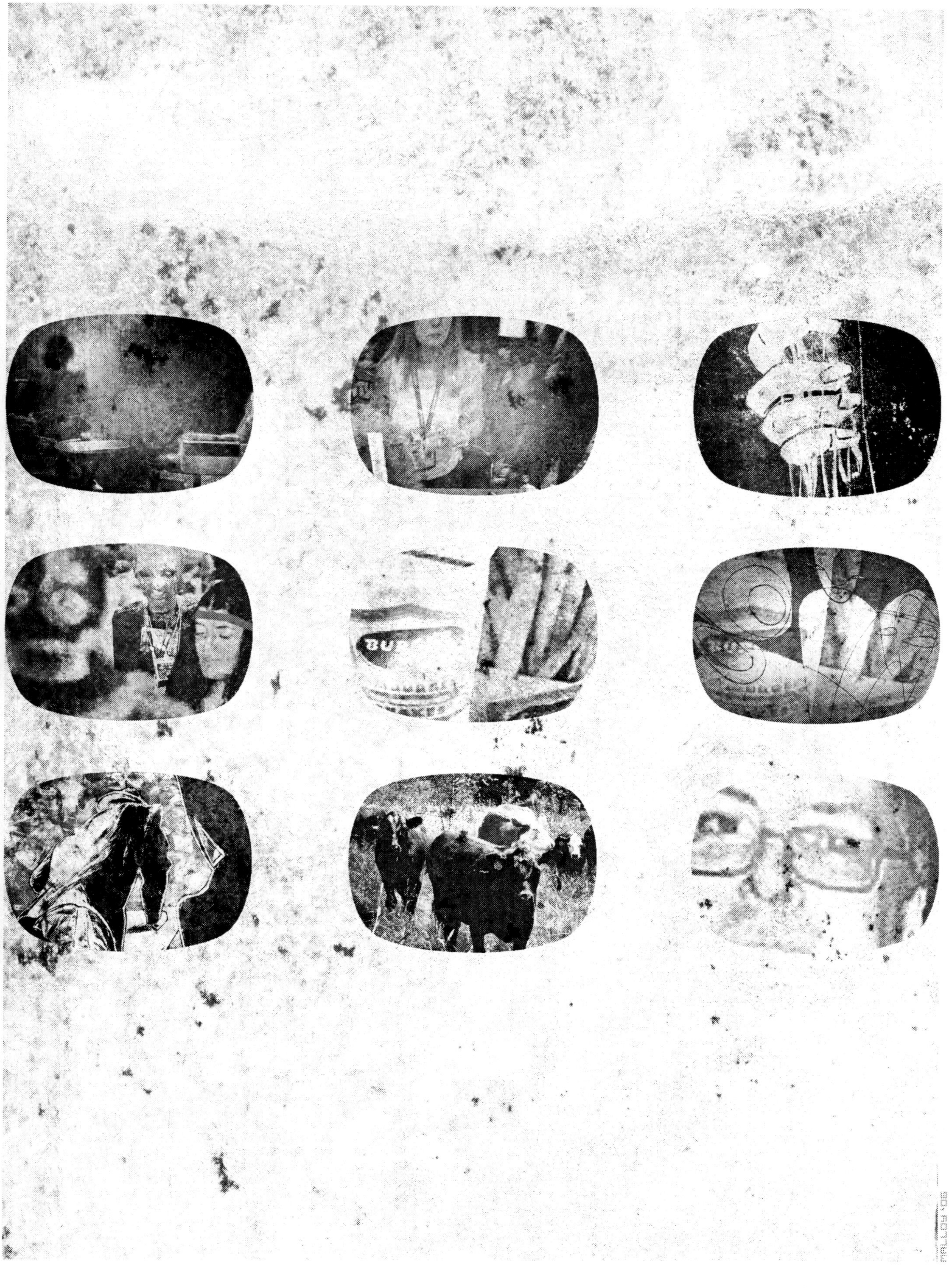
MALLOY '08

"We know of only one man who has direct knowledge of this very dark and disturbing era in black operations. He is a man who is purported to have lived many lives... ladies and gentlemen, please welcome Mr. Al Leedskalnin!" Just as the audience begins to clap, Al receives a devastating blue arch in his arm. He grabs onto it, grimacing with pain, that goddamn horrible streak of pain. Peabody sees the arch shoot out from behind the curtain and knows something's up. Only Damon actually witnessed the arch. He just stands there, offstage, staring at Al with his mouth open and a confused look etched upon his face. Al gathers himself, steadies, and moves out to the stage still

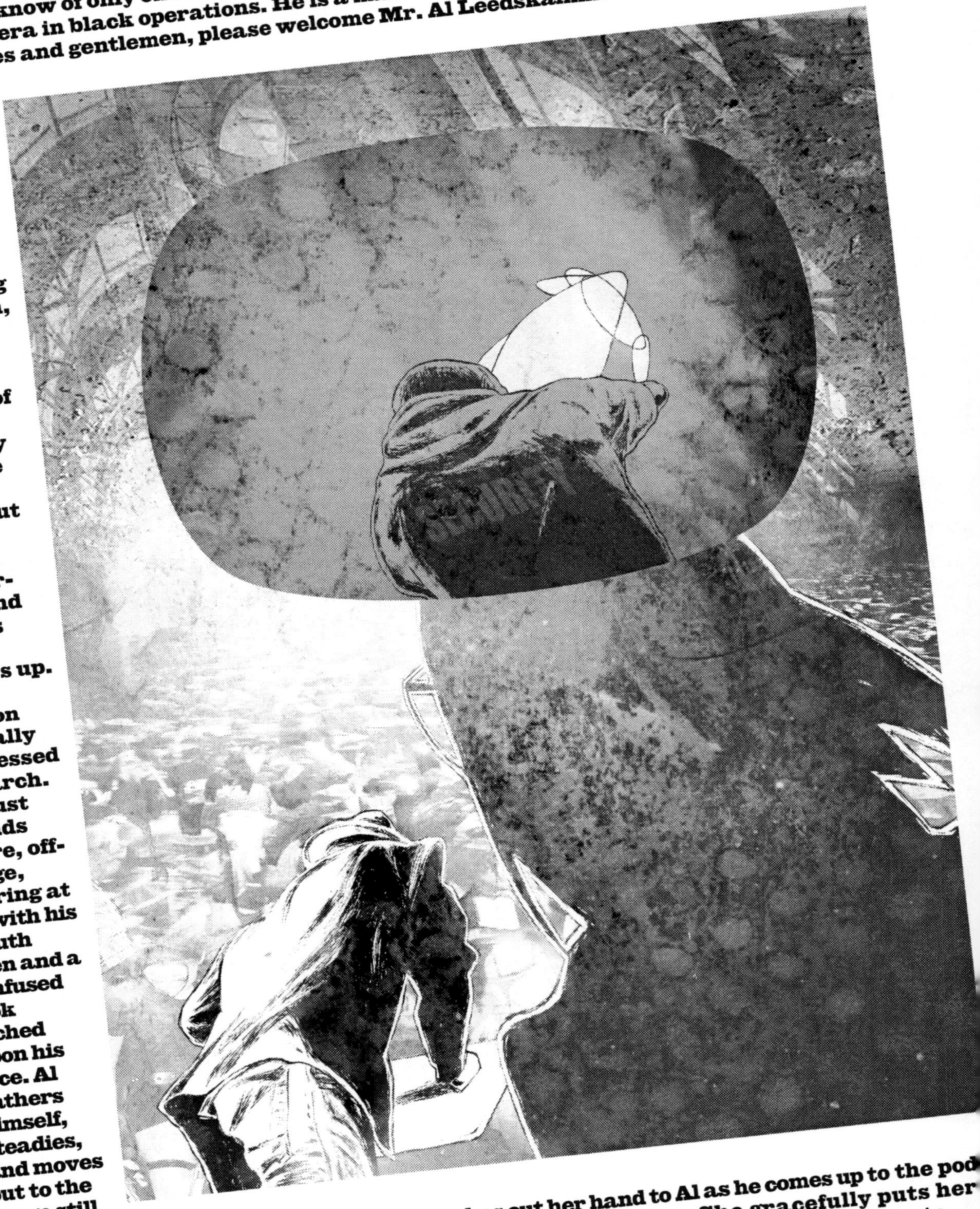

holding onto his right arm. Ms. Wexler reaches out her hand to Al as he comes up to the podium but he just grimaces. He can't raise it. It hurts too much. She gracefully puts her hand to his shoulder and smiles. Al walks up to the podium stretching a little to address the crowd as if to speak into the microphone. He doesn't realize that the microphone is on his lapel. He stretches his neck like a rubber chicken and says,

Thanks for coming... grkkkkkkkk... grkkkkkkkk... uhhhhhhh... Grkkkk-rkkkkkk...." Al starts time-glitching, and the sound is unnerving, making a distinct echo in the arena. Peabody is sweating and beginning to panic. Al looks out into the audience with a slightly confused look. Then, just in time, Ms. Wexler interrupts the awkward moment and says, "Please, let's sit down. There's so much to discuss." Ms. Wexler points to the two mauve-colored seats in the middle of the stage, and motions for them to sit down.

Before they settle in, Al is a little distracted as he looks about the crowd for Peabody. Al sees him and motions to him. Ms. Wexler dives in quite seriously, saying "Mr. Leedskalnin, I'd like to start with Project Window Shade. Back in the early '70's, this was a government funded program which finally came to light in 1985, when the Rosenberg Files were brought forth by Stanley Rosenberg, former assistant secretary to Admiral Haute. A copy of the file was sent to myself and other researchers, and quite honestly, we all thought it was another very clever debunking effort simply because of what it entailed. But after several months of research into these papers, we actually found that they were consistent with other military and intelligence documents of that time period. We've found that the documents revealed a working co-operation of several special interest groups into the area of consciousness itself, not just UFO's. There are many theories of course, including the most popular theory if you will, that this and other projects were developed to work with the grey's to help solve their reproduction dilemma. In return, we would receive advanced technology. Mr Leedskalnin, what can you tell us of Project Window Shade?"

At that very moment, the two clones burst onto the stage. The tall one is shrieking, "UNGAWWWWWWWW UNAGAWWWWWWW!" The shorter of the two addresses the crowd, muttering, "KILL Morris K. Jessup! KILL Morris K. Jessup! Eat at Kentucky Fried Chicken! Save more at BestBuy! KILL Morris K. Jessup! Freemasons rule the world! STaRbUcks!" Ms. Wexler is appropriately alarmed by this intrusion as are Damon, Al, and Peabody. The crowd of UFO fanatics think that it's all part of the presentation, they begin to laugh and guffaw. As the Al clone continues his unearthly shrieking, "KILL MOrris K. JesSup! Vidal Sasoon... I smell Sex and Candy! Kill Morris K. Jessup! Eat Burger King! Kill Morris K. JesSup!" the shrieking becomes excruciating. Finally, two security guards make it to the stage and struggle to escort the two clones to the green room, but not without great difficulty. "Kill Morris K. Jessup! CONTAINERS! CONTAIN-ERS! YOU'RE ALL CONTAINERS!" they continue. Al just looks over at Peabody, who is shaking his head back and forth in denial. He's looking down at the ground in shame. There is a deafening silence after this bizarre event, returning the focus on Al. "GRKKKKKK... grkkkkKKkk kkk...."

Al stands completely silent after the schizophrenic episode, when finally Ms. Wexler, somewhat frazzled, says, "Well that was interesting!" with a half smile. She's attempting to make light of the situation and console the crowd as the scattered uncomfortable laughter from the audience dissi-pates. She is at a loss to regain her composure when Al returns to his senses and politely commands, "Ms. Wexler, please sit down. I'm going to tell you some things. You might not believe what I'm going to tell you, but nonethe-less, it's what I know. I... only ask that you don't bog down what I'm about to reveal with circular, rhetorical logic in the quest for scientific proof and veri-fication. That's 99% of the problem you see. That's the main reason humans do not progress. They only delude themselves that they are progressing when all the while they are blinded by their self imposed ignorance, reinforced by the use, or in this case, the abuse, of technology.

Now, let me tell you about your aliens..."

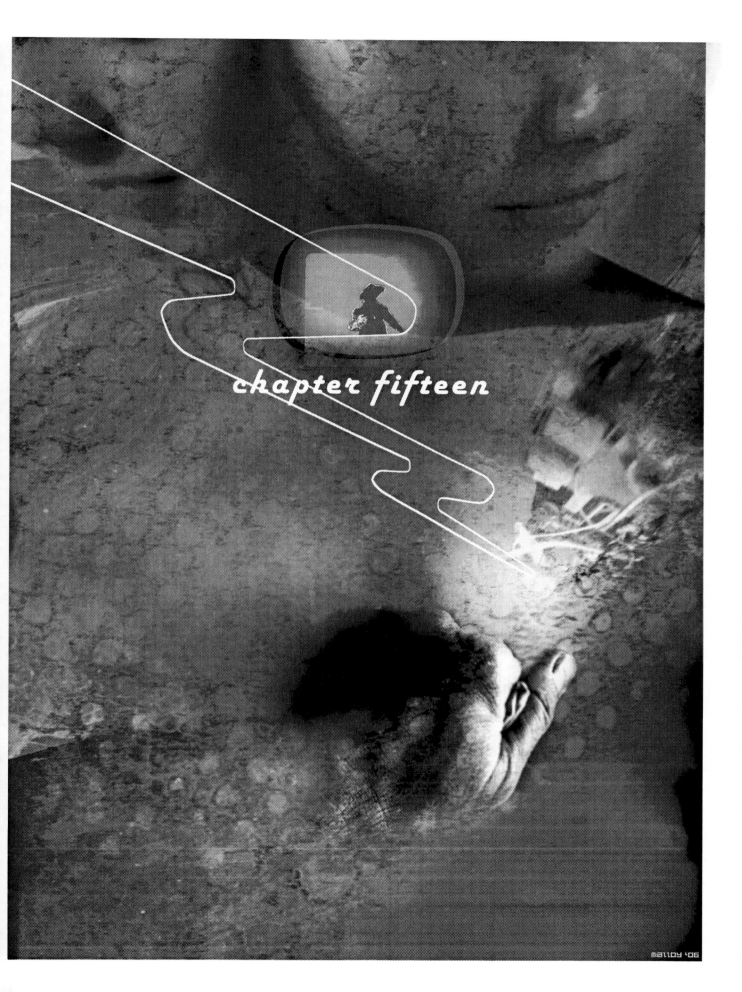

chapter fifteen

malloy '06

There is an anxious silence over the auditorium. It's as if the presence of something ancient has been revealed and all present are about to witness the most important event in their lives. Al stares at Ms. Wexler for a moment, seemingly to gather his thoughts and reflect, and then proceeds, "Errr... Ms. Wexler, the "aliens", for lack of a better term, are hoping to inherit the earth very soon... as it's actually their turn, you see. You're all living on borrowed time." Barbara Wexler looks at Al for several seconds, clearly reeling, but finds refuge in her journalistic instincts, asking, "Why? What exactly do you mean, Mr. Leedskalnin?" "Oh, please my dear, its all so very obvious at this point. The humans are lost... cocooned in their everyday patterns of going to and fro, identifying with and consuming products and information of irrelevance. They heed signals and words that have no foundation, you... you've become completely separated from what's truly going on around you, to what's right in front of you! One cannot truly make the journey to find the truth while clinging to things of delusion. Even the Pope will tell you that Ms. Wexler. I ask you, why would human history suddenly not repeat itself, with society after society ending in ruin? It's no different anywhere in the world at any point in time. Humans are repeatedly prone to fail, to break down, and ultimately destroy themselves. Can't we ALL see that humans don't belong? Is it not completely obvious? Are humans REALLY that stupid?" Al pauses, and says, "I'm sorry... Ms. Wexler, I get carried away... let me continue...

...please."

Al actually relaxes a little, as all in attendance cling to his every word. He finally settles into his newfound element. "While it is true that Tesla was channeling a distinct intelligence, he wasn't the first," he says, "It's been happening for millennia, you see. The information Tesla received is radiating throughout the cosmos and is simultaneously at the very core of all information based organisms. In fact, it's really what's behind the many mysteries of the world. How do you suppose *Sumeria*[1] appeared out of nowhere, with no predecessor? Where do you think the knowledge to build the great pyramid and all that it represents came from? How is it that the Mayan calendar is still unchallenged as a perfect, infinite mathematical calendar? I can go on and on... but you get my drift. It's all right there in front of you and has been for so long that nobody knows the difference anymore. The people of the world have had blinders on for so long my dear, that even a little bit of light is painful now." Al pauses.

His brows begin to knit as he says, "Ms. Wexler, people feel that something is wrong. They say that time is moving too fast, and well... that's because it is. In the '70's everything had hit full stride and the tipping point was firmly established. It's been mounting ever since we dropped those damn Nazi bombs out there in the desert... those CRUDE LITTLE EARMARKS OF OUR STATUS HERE ON EARTH!!"

Al explodes in disgust before continuing, saying, "Ms. Wexler, if the earth is 4 billion years old, which doesn't really mean anything in the grand scheme... but even if it was just ONE million years old... why, there is simply no example of the kind of acceleration you have experienced in the last 100!"

I. SUMER [Shumer, Sumeria, Shinar, native ki-en-gir]: an area in the southern region of Babylonia in present-day Iraq that flowered a highly advanced culture during the 4th millenium B.C. Sumerian pre-cuneiform scripts precede any other form of writing.

"I mean, jet propulsion, semi-conductors, microchips, laser beams, fiber optics, stealth technology, nuclear fission, DNA! Not to mention burning fuel and rubber on an unprecedented scale! All in THE LAST 100 YEARS! My GOD people! WAKE UP!" Al exclaims, slowly shaking his head. Then, he gently explains..."Why, Ms. Wexler, that isn't even a thousandth of a grain of sand on all the beaches of the earth in reference t marking time by even the most advanced methods. There is no relationship between spirituality and technology. We've lost our way, and the descent actually started a lor time ago."

"The people who run the planet... the World Bank, the IMF, you name it, they know that history has been ending ever since. They know, by the reports that cross their desks, about the ever-expanding ozone hole, the toxicification o the oceans, the effects of clearing the rain forests, and most relevantly, the end all *Novelty*[1]. They know that our societies cannot sustain themselves. The earth is bursting at the seams with human madness, Ms. Wexler. Einstein was right or the money with events, but it's all really so much stranger than that. We've got far bigger problems than grey alien folks, trust me."

The earth is reaching a point of resonance, a critical point in the time wave. What's happening is not only is time moving too fast, technology itself is moving too fast and is completely out of control. More importantly, the novelty of all things human is coming to an end... meaning, there is limited potential for further creationism of the human container. Redundancy spells disaster, Ms. Wexler. WE are responsible for the acceleration of our own extermination, can you not see that? Things are badly out of whack. WAY out of whack my dear. Coincidences and synchronicities are randomly glitching all over the time wave, even as we speak. The governments of the world have been covertly chasing the accidents and mistakes for decades, and there's no real way to stop it.

Soon, very soon, the past, present, and future will all merge into a finite point and no-one, and I mean NO-ONE, knows what the outcome will be. We DO know that there are good and malevolent intelligences involved, that are both highly concerned and motivated by their own needs of survival."

I. NOVELTY: The late writer and philosopher, Terence McKenna, argued that time itself was nothing more than a fractal wave of "*novelty*", or the introduction of new ideas and change-producing events. According to McKenna, this wave is in a process of collapsing to a *zero point*.

"Ms. Wexler, the people must prepare for the coming change."

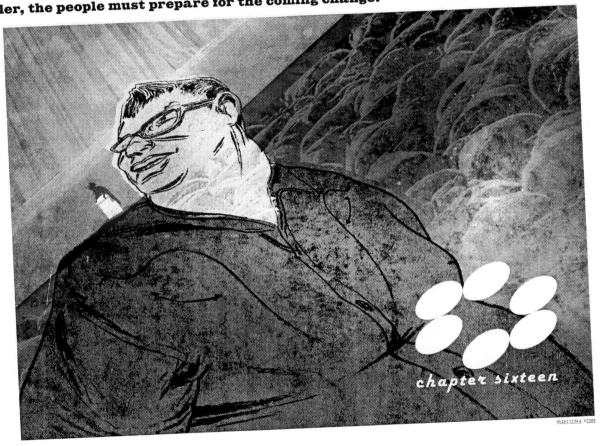

chapter sixteen

For the first time in her career, Ms. Wexler doesn't know what to say. After a brief moment of silence, the attendees begin to applaud. Their handclaps get louder and louder until the entire audience stands up. Peabody looks around to try and determine what's happening, expecting more clones or worse. It soon becomes apparent that they are actually applauding Al. He has deeply moved the crowd. Ms. Wexler and Damon are equally moved as well by Al's honesty. Peabody can't believe it. He looks around the auditorium and for the first time in a long time, starts smiling, grinning from ear to ear. It's like a weight has been lifted. He steps out to see behind him as the crowd continues applauding. He then looks proudly to Al, who's mildly glitching, Peabody reminds himself he'll need the device again but doesn't let this effect the moment.

There is a definite sense of urgency to the auditorium. The **UFOCON** attendees are now looking to **Al** for direction. He feels a little like a movie star as a result of the adulation. He approaches the podium, again extending his neck to reach the microphone, and says, "Go home to your loved ones. Say the things you want to say and do the things you want to do. For you, it's easy. Just do the right things, stick to the highest ground... affect people in your immediate influence positively! That's all anyone really ever needed to do. **Do NOT** try to save the planet with that bleeding heart drama queen buffoonery... that's a futile waste of thought and energy. Just take action where you can actually make an impact." For myself and Mr. Freeman, its not so easy, but good luck to you all."

Al exits the noisy auditorium stage left. Peabody knows he's going for the closest exit so they can get back out there, back in the field, regardless of what it may bring. Peabody cuts across the emerging sea of people nodding to his new-found fans and smiles curtly, hearing praises like, "Thank you Mr. Freeman! Thank you." Peabody feels an overwhelming guilt and knows there might not be much time left for any of them. Little do they know that he is responsible for unleashing an unfathomable force that is destroying the earth in the most unthinkable way, by slowly erasing it. He almost has to remind himself about how the advanced technology was disseminated into the global corporations of the world, for "socio-economic advancement", and that there were no instructions. Therefore, there were many mistakes, including the accidental creation of a miniature black hole the size of a pinhead. Essentially, an infinitely small amount of incredibly dense matter was accidentally shifted from one state to another. It then manifested itself into this dimension or reality. Releasing anti-matter, it propels itself through the earth every day or two like a bullet, rocketing out one side until hitting peak velocity, then suspends in orbit for a while before falling back in the opposite direction and doing it all over again. It zigzags the globe, erasing matter in its wake. The real problem is that it's getting bigger every time this occurs and it will eventually consume the planet if unstopped.

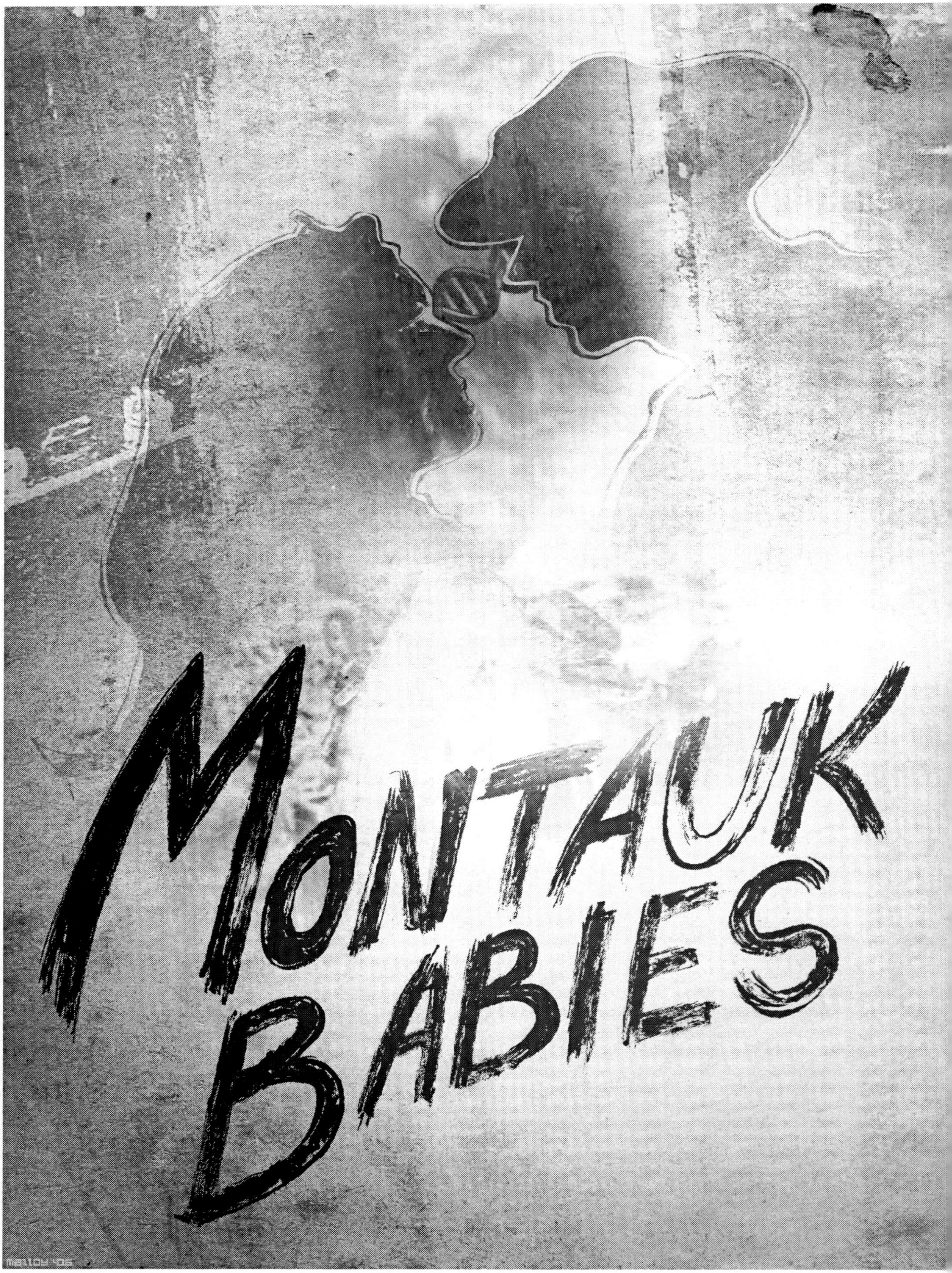
MONTAUK
BABIES
malloy '05

Ms. Wexler calls out for Al amidst the cacophony as he scrambles toward the emergency exit door. When he opens the door, an ethereal ray of sunlight beams across the auditorium from the scorching desert outside. "Mr. Leedskalnin," she says, "Thank you... I... I." "Oh please my dear, call me Al," he replies, "You and Damon take care now." "But," says Ms. Wexler. Peabody slams the door behind them and says, "Al, what are we going to do, huh? If the clones aren't dealt with, they might kill someone or worse." "Won't be the first time kid, we need to determine the status of the problem. Stay Vector, anything can happen Freeman...

...anything," says Al.

chapter seventeen

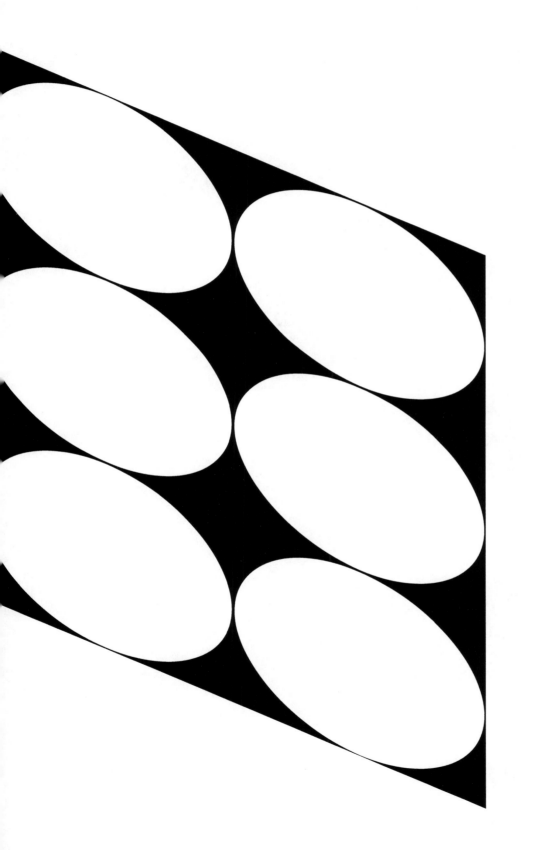

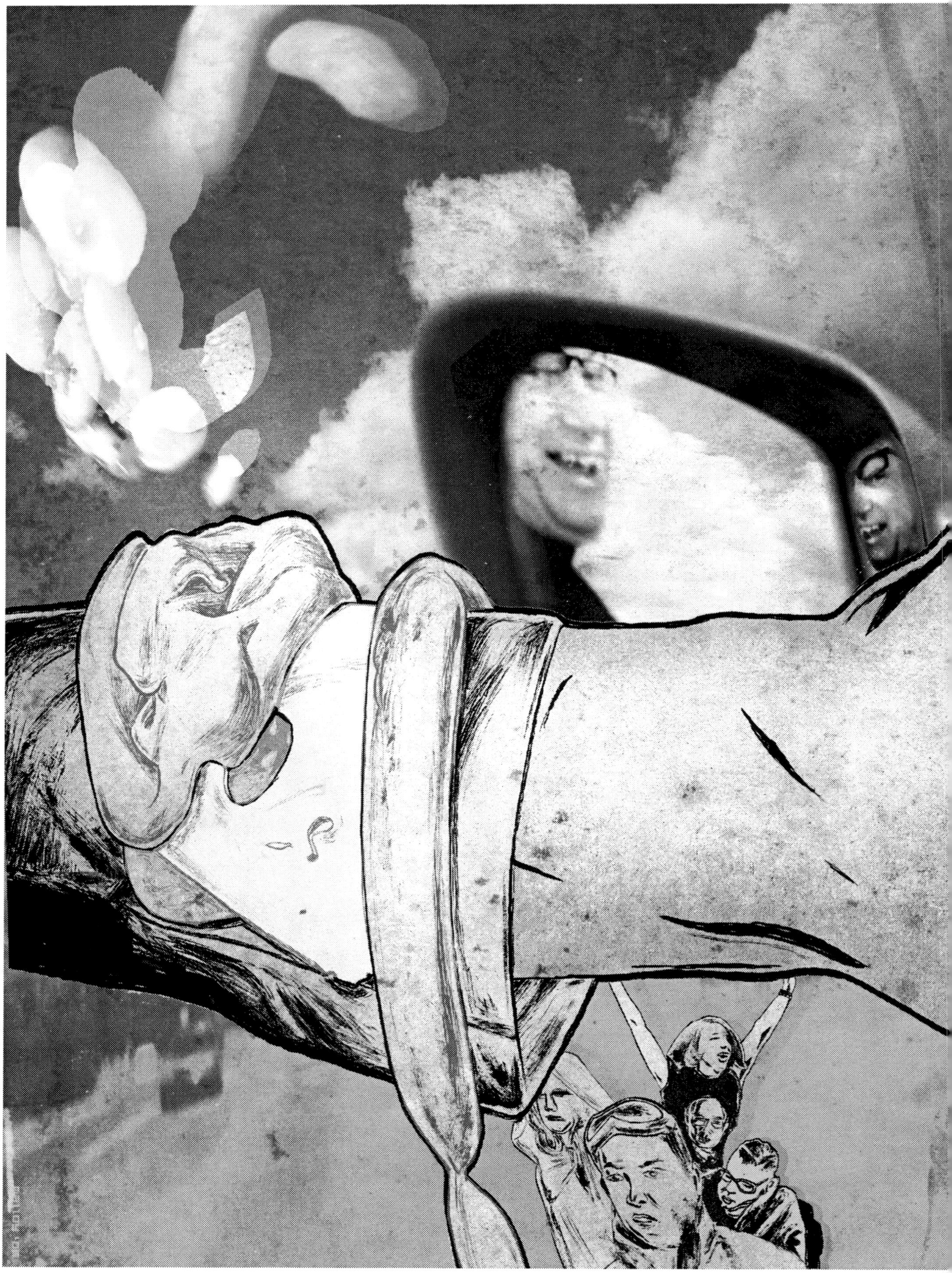

In the parking lot, Peabody realizes that they don't have access to the Buick. This is exactly the kind of thing Peabody fears most, being detained or getting in some kind of situation that would prevent them from performing accident duty. He knows they need to get out of there and that there are clones in the area. Al slyly produces a key to the shuttle van and says, "Lifted it just in case. Did I tell you about when we used to pick pockets near Cannery Row?" Peabody forces himself into the driver's seat of the shuttle van and proceeds to wrestle their way out of the now swarming parking lot. Just as they near the exit, the homunculus Peabody clone runs straight at the shuttle van! He is repulsively gnawing his teeth on the windshield with a loud, violent SPLATT! He hurdles himself onto the windshield and grasping out for Al and Peabody through the side windows in a desperate attempt to get at them. The Al clone is close behind screaming, "UNGAWWWWWW... KILL! KILL! KILL! Morris K. Jessup! KILL Morris K. Jessup! UNGaaWWWW!" He is covered in lunchmeat, cheeses and assorted deli items from the struggle in the green room. As the Al clone grabs for Peabody through the driver's side window, the material spews everywhere violently. The scene is disturbing at best. "CoNTaINeRS! YoU're All ConTainerS!" screams the Al clone. A throng of sci-fi geeks swarms the clones. One bespectacled conventioneer wearing Spock ears senses the danger and pulls out a jumbo pepper spray, yelling, "Get back! GET BACK!" He blasts the clones directly in the face as Al and Peabody escape. They start gasping like strange fish out water. It's a mortifying site, as they gasp deeper and harder, it becomes apparent that they aren't human. Finally, Peabody makes it onto the 375.

"Why did you have to go and do that Al? What good will it do?" whines Peabody. "Aw, c'mon Freeman. What does it really matter at this point? We've given them some peace of mind for show of their lives. It's what they've all longed for. We save them the show of their lives. It's what they've all longed for. I couldn't bear to tell them that it could be over in just hours. Hell, the way I see it, it's all been a freebie for them anyway!" The excitement triggers him to glitch, "GRKKKKKK... grkkkkKKkk kkk... Al knows he needs the device but shrugs it off. Peabody is disgruntled because they've lost their groove, they need to get back on track or his life will have been a complete and total waste. Peabody knows that the accident is only one of many problems facing the earth actually, but nonetheless he is driven to NOT make his life a failure. Al stare forward and just says, "NORTH! IT'S NORTH, FREEMAN!" They continue up the 375 and drive... same as it ever was.

There was a time, long ago, when Al figured he was a grey himself. Not knowing any different, he was kept in the same holding tank for years. This partially explains his strange affinity for them, as well as his awkwardness among humans. He knows that the greys have fears like humans do, and that they don't exactly have feelings... but want to. The truth is that most of the alien species don't know who or what God is either, nor do they know where they themselves come from, let alone where we come from. They are eons removed from their origins, just as we are.

Al has nothing to go on. He's received no mental images, no tips, no nothing. He feels like an empty receptacle. He starts to lose faith as it turns to dusk. The two-lane freeway seems to go on forever. Finally, a soft dew descends upon the windshield of the shuttle van. Peabody rolls down his window and pulls out one of the instruments from his pocket protector. Holding it out the window for a few seconds, he pulls his heavy arm back into the vehicle, but not before bumping his hand on the window guard. "Positive orgone is 2.7," he says, "no doubt we're in the right area."

They see orange lights in the distance that career off to the east, where the pavement ends at the end of the valley. They stop where they saw the lights. It becomes dark and they need to use the headlights to look for a tip on where it'll come down. Al hurries out to a high point. With the desert wind blowing his jacket flaps, he holds onto his black derby. He looks around in all directions for a sign, so they can get there in time (they weren't always as good at accident duty as they are now... there have been times when they've been off by a few miles). Not bad considering the size of the earth, but leaving even the tiniest hole unattended for too long would simply be disastrous. Every second is precious on accident duty. The Ea started giving Al tips in the form of mental images as their concerns became more and more grave. Because Al is not exactly human himself, this does not technically violate any intervention guidelines they've imposed on themselves. It's a cosmic loophole if you will. Where there's a will, there's a way.

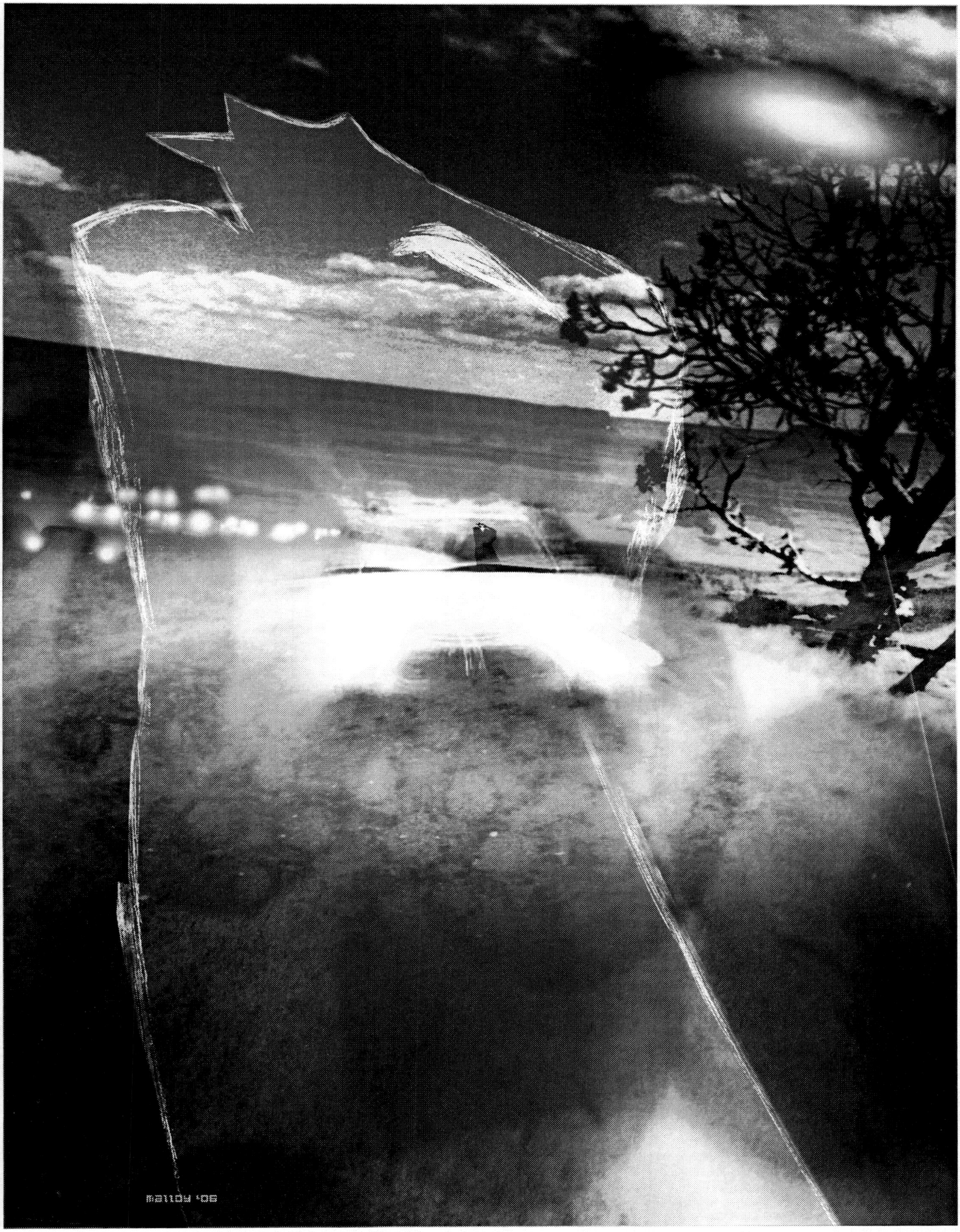
malloy '06

This time however, it's different. Al is concerned that he hasn't received anything from the Ea at all, zero in fact. He stands defiantly on a desert mound, desperately scanning the area while clinging to his dream of a normal life, somehow, someway. Without it, he has nothing. Just before he is about to give in and collapse, Peabody exclaims, "AL! OVER THERE!" Looking south, Al sees several orange lights dancing back and forth at ground level. They are both riveted by the lights, until finally, engine noise can be heard. It's apparent that the lights are actually headlights and there are dozens of them coming their way up the dirt road. Peabody reacts, "OH GREAT! THAT'S GREAT! WHAT THE HELL IS GOING ON!?" "Don't know kid," replies Al, "don't know." Finally, a yellow Humvee, with every bell and whistle imaginable, pulls up next to the Buick with a blanket of dust being raised by the countless vehicles behind it. Hurriedly, a short man about 5 feet tall, wearing camouflage fatigues, emerges from the gaudy vehicle and races towards them, breathing heavily. "Mr. Leedskalnin!" he says, "Mr. Freeman! I'm Matt Clarksdale of the Infinity UFO Group. We're here in a show of support to assist you in anyway we can! We've detained those two assailants back at the convention center. It appears that the power grid is going out across the country... probably around the world. The military and DOD are not reacting to anything. It seems like everything is shutting down! Mr. Leedskalnin, what   can   we   do   to   help?"

chapter eighteen

Al is furious. "The first thing you can do is get the hell out of here!" he growls, "You damn kids will ruin our chances, this is no place for humans! Don't you understand? I know you kids mean well but you've GOT TO GO!" There are vehicles everywhere. Dust is billowing over the entire area. Hundreds of conventioneers are getting out of the cars, trying to see what's going on. As the dust begins to settle, Peabody notices that there are dew drops on Matt Clarkdale's glasses. The atmosphere is rapidly becoming moist. Peabody looks up instinctively, and says, "Al... its too late... they're... they're here." The sky above is scattered with enormous UFO's slowly moving in on them from every direction. They make no sound as they move closer, they look more like clouds than machines. They are so immense that the sci-fi geeks are completely and totally awestruck. Peabody himself is caught up in the gnosis, when Al barks, "Freeman! Snap out of it! That's what they do. They put the humans in a trance. C'mon, snap out of it Freeman! This is our shot kid! GET IT TOGETHER!" Peabody rolls his body back and forth as if he's wrapped tightly with cellophane and trying to break loose. Al dashes over and slaps Peabody in the face three times, while all the conventioneers stand motionless. Peabody has inadvertently built up some resistance and is able to shake off the gnosis. He quickly grabs the device out of his duffle bag.

Al assumes they are trying to show them the position and bolts as fast as he can towards the center of the configuration. There are exactly 12 of the immense ships moving together forming a circle, resulting in a huge, geodesic pattern in the sky. He runs with total commitment in his awkward, straight up posture, occasionally cupping his derby. Peabody is fighting to move as quickly as possible behind Al, giving it everything he's got. Within seconds, he's perspiring. Al shouts out, "Get ready freeman! Get ready!!" Looking up through the hole in the sky left by the UFO's, Al sees a huge arching ball, now the size of an aircraft carrier. It gets bigger and bigger as it descends rapidly towards them, blocking out the night sky. Al screams, "My God! My dear, dear God, Freeman! It's HUGE! Get ready, Freeman!" And then...

FWAAABBOOOSH

FWAAABBOOOSHaaaaaaaaaa

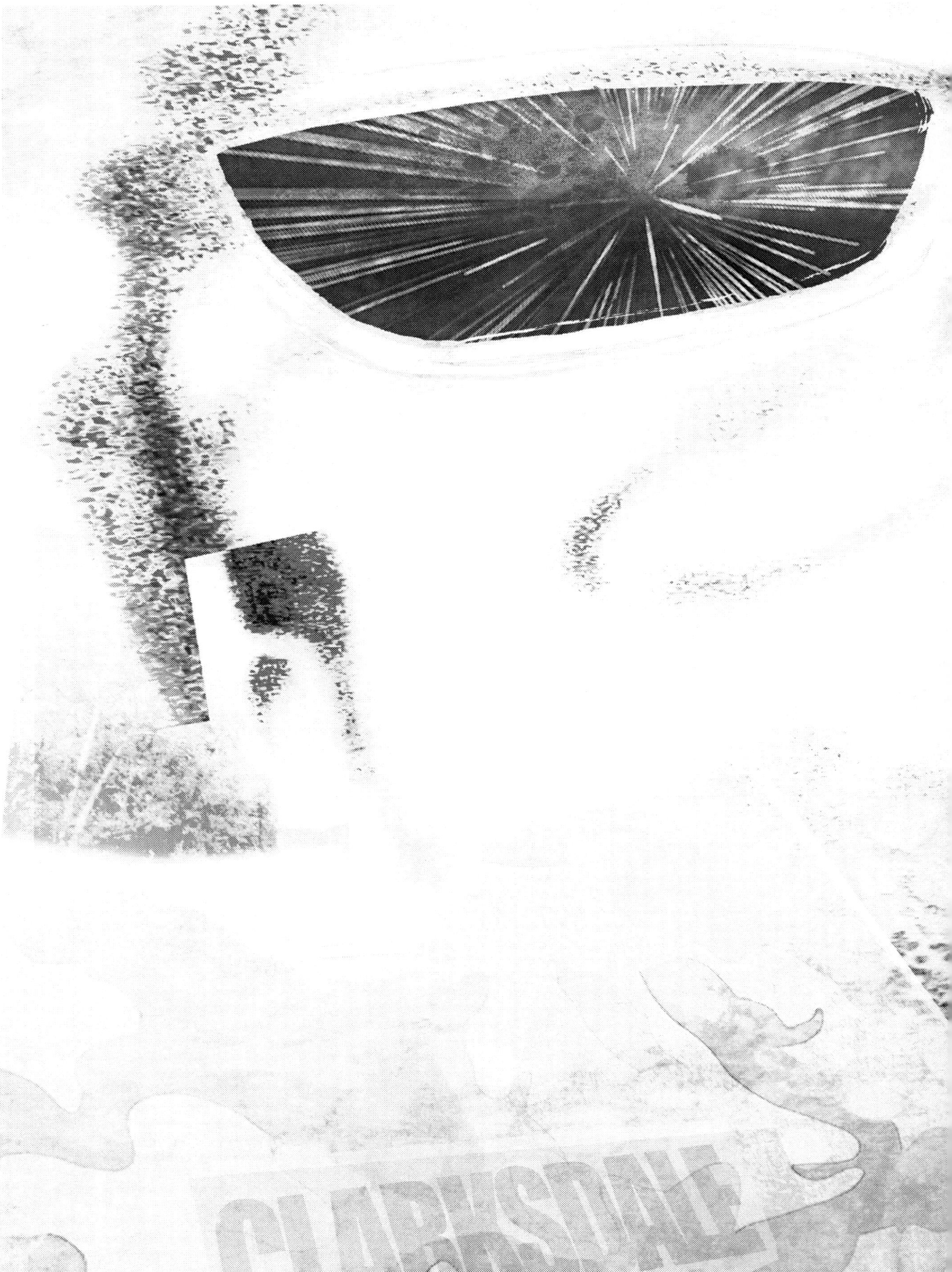

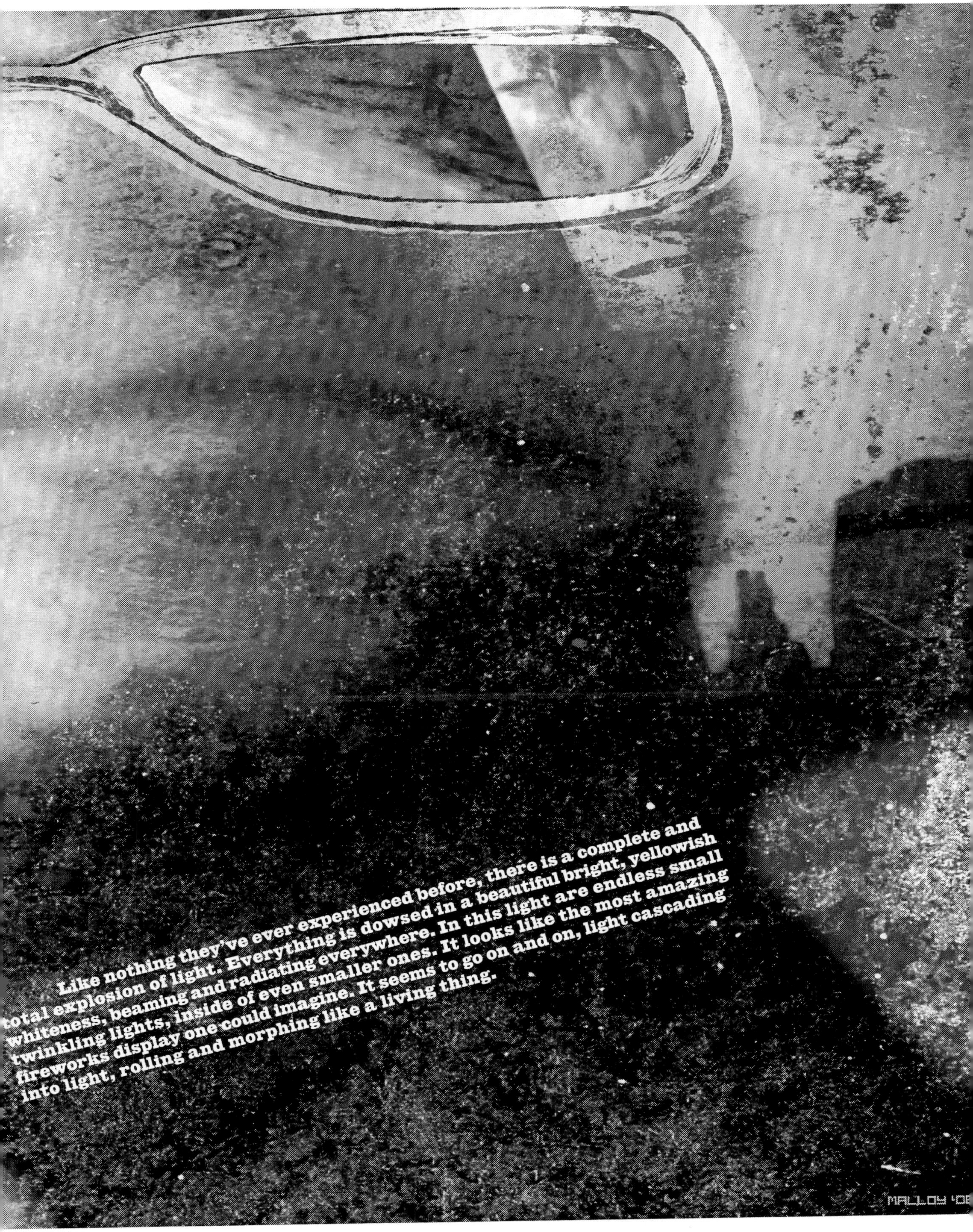
MALLOY '0

Like nothing they've ever experienced before, there is a complete and total explosion of light. Everything is dowsed in a beautiful bright, yellowish whiteness, beaming and radiating everywhere. In this light are endless small twinkling lights, inside of even smaller ones. It looks like the most amazing fireworks display one could imagine. It seems to go on and on, light cascading into light, rolling and morphing like a living thing.

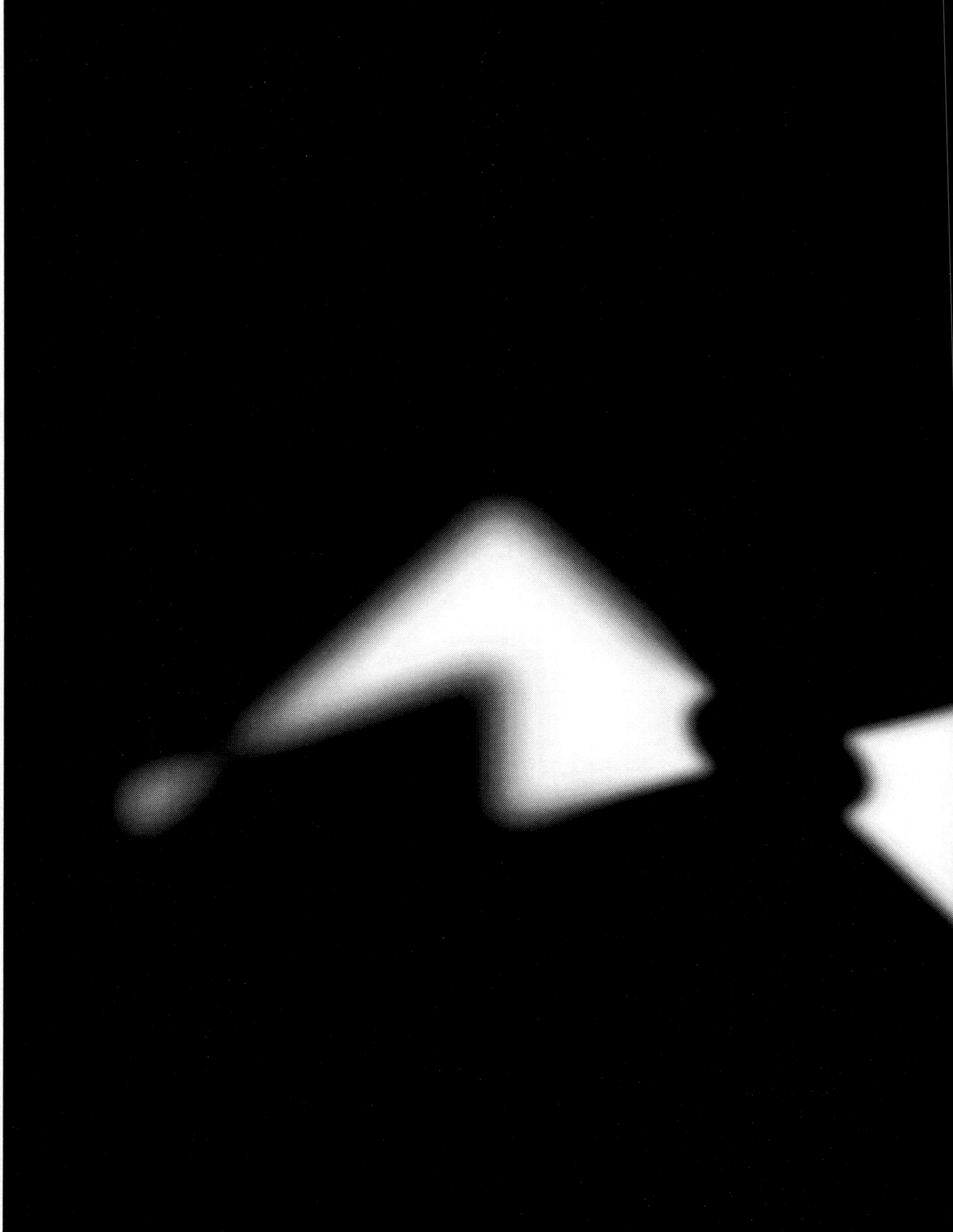

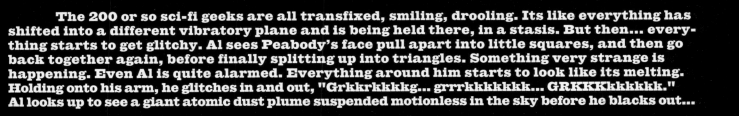

The 200 or so sci-fi geeks are all transfixed, smiling, drooling. Its like everything has shifted into a different vibratory plane and is being held there, in a stasis. But then... everything starts to get glitchy. Al sees Peabody's face pull apart into little squares, and then go back together again, before finally splitting up into triangles. Something very strange is happening. Even Al is quite alarmed. Everything around him starts to look like its melting. Holding onto his arm, he glitches in and out, "Grkkrkkkkg... grrrkkkkkkk... GRKKKkkkkkk." Al looks up to see a giant atomic dust plume suspended motionless in the sky before he blacks out...

A horned toad peers into Al's face as the merciless sun creeps under his eyelids. He slowly comes to, spitting out the dry, brown dust that he's been laying in all night. The toad hops off, chasing a beetle with the vigor of an escaped prisoner. Far behind Al is Peabody. He's lying on his back, his sizable torso burgeoning in the crisp, blue sunlight. "Ungghh... ungghh...", he groans. Al struggles to get his bearings and says, "Freeman. Freeman. C'mon, get up. Let's move. C'mon kid." Their bones crack in sync as they shake the dust from their limbs.

Browning saw everything from his RV trance. His whole life has been something of a

chapter nineteen

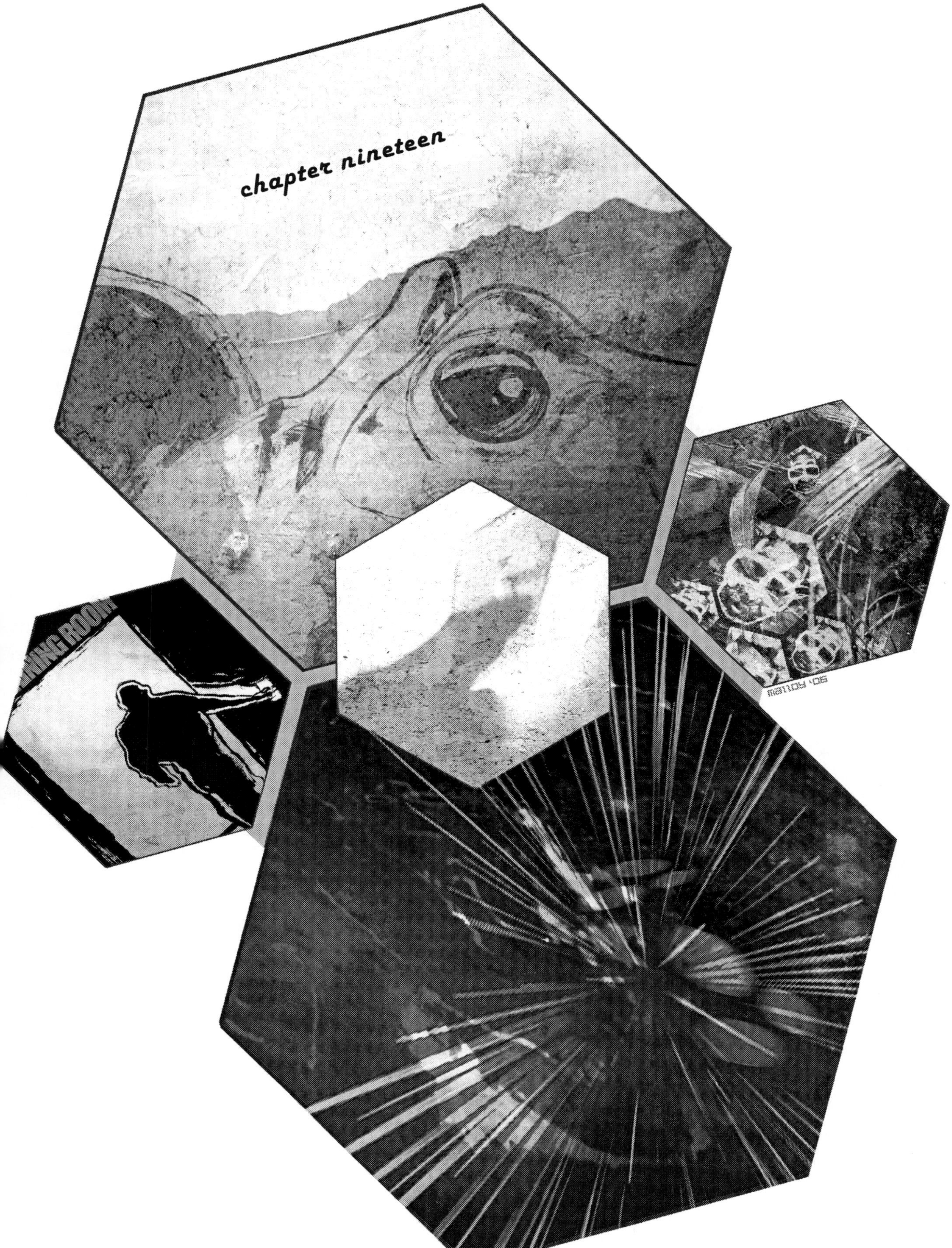

cruel journey, an endless series of turns and twists of which he's had no control. In the end it's something that makes him truly unique. He's the only one who really knows what happened out there in the desert. Aside from Al, he's the only one who will remember seeing the massive Ea ships for that matter. Due to his disembodied state, he was unaffected by the gnosis they radiate. He witnessed the accident, with all its inherent energy and matter dissipate into nothingness, obliterated by a precise, opposing force equal to it in all ways. "The Ea must deal with similar matters in deep space," he thinks to himself. Little does he know that they have actually created planets this way. Regardless, he understands, as much as the Shaman, that what we think are distant stars are really much more a part of us than we realize, and that the time has come for another great change. A great shift is happening. It's a gift from the highest order of the cosmos. His mission will serve to help others relate, and adapt, to what will be - a very different world.

Peabody is up and about, looking disheveled to say the least. His hair sticks up on one side of his head, and the tops of his large buttocks are visible above his belt line. Ignoring his discomfort, he uses his *multi-spectrometer*[1] to find that the readings are all over the map. A wanders about with small rocks imbedded in his tired, black jacket, which is painted in streaks of the brown, shiny dust. "What's that kid?" he asks. "There must be something wrong with the calibration," Peabody says, "I... I... can't seem to get a true reading, no matter what setting I use. If this is accurate, then nothing electro-magnetic should be able to work! Al, this is impossible... it can't be true! It's like... hey! UFO MAN! You here? Anybody home?"

Matt Clarksdale sticks his head out of the window of the yellow Humvee and waves at Peabody, still higher than high from the gnosis. "Tuuurn your raaadio onnnn!" Peabody commands, "turn on The Radio!" "Okay! Ok!", Clarksdale finally responds, "Its just, just this noise, schhhhhhhhh, like that!" Peabody anxiously exclaims, "ALL the channels!?" After a few seconds, Matt Clarksdale shouts from the Humvee, "Yeah, every single one of them!" "Al! Al! Something's happened!" shouts Peabody, "SOMETHING AMAZING HAPPENED LAST NIGHT! Look... I don't believe it. There's no trace of a hole. Something tells me the problem has been disposed of. No hole. No hole, no hole..... no hole."

"Al, look!" Peabody yips as he points out to the desert, where the hole should have been. Al scopes the topography with his keener eye and says, "I think you're right Freeman. Something happened alright... you've lost your mind once again!"

I. SPECTROMETER: A Spectroscope equipped with scales for measuring wavelengths or indexes-of-refraction of multiple kinds.

Al marches back to the shuttle van, followed directly by Peabody, who is still crunching numbers and doing tests with his pocket Nephelometer[1]. Catching up with Al, Peabody reports, "I think I know what happened. You won't believe this, but turn on the radio." "C'mon, Freeman," Al says, "I feel like crap. I'm tired of being here and I'm tired of your... mmm... just get me to a Motel6, pronto!" he barks. "Alright chief, but first turn on the damn radio... PWETTY PWEEEEASE." Al leans over, disgusted and momentarily guilt-ridden at the same time, and begrudgingly turns the knob. "Nothin! Just noise Freeman," he says. "Try the other channels Al. You can do it," Peabody replies. "hssshshshs shhhhhhhh ksshh-hhhhh, fhooooosssshh..." "Very funny. They're all bad kid, who cares?" Al retorts. "Al, listen to me for once..." Peabody pleads, "I think that the problem has been eliminated by a perfectly directed amount of equal energy done in such a way as to only destroy the target. I think we were in the middle of a controlled explosion, equivalent to a mini Big Bang. Don't you get it? The residual effects of this will make it impossible for electromagnetic waves to travel from point A to point B. The electromagnetic spectrum will be too unstable to coherently transmit any kind of signal!" Peabody can hardly contain his excitable nature, and keeps going, "THERE WILL BE NO TELEVISION! NO RADIO ! NO CELL PHONES! NO TRANMSITTER OR RECEIVER CAN FUNCTION! Al, it could be a thousand years before all this settles down. Don't you see?"

Al Leedskalnin stoically looks off in the opposite direction, toward the mountains. He then looks back to where the hole should have been. Finally, it all dawns on him. "Freeman!" he says, "My god, man! It's true. It makes perfect sense. I should have listened to you in the first place. Everybody will have to start over. They'll be cut off from the very thing that has dictated the steadfast decline of the last 100 years! My god! They'll have to start over from scratch! It's a miracle, Freeman! A MIRACLE, I TELL YOU!" Not missing a beat, Al decides, "Freeman, we've got to get out of here! Do you remember that place in Idaho? The one by that river where the water was so clean and pure and where you could see the moon shinin' down on you like a good old friend? Let's go kid! Lets go! Our work here is done my boy. It's time for us to live it up! It's a re-do Freeman, a RE-DO!!"

They look at each other. Peabody puts the spectrometer back in his pocket protector and says, "No. I mean, ...you're right, our work is done. I can hardly believe it myself. But I hate Idaho. Let's go to the Adirondacks. It's a hell of a lot cleaner." Now, for the first time, Al finds himself truly at a loss. He fidgets with his hat, stares at the ground, the sky, at anything but Peabody. After a deep breath he looks Freeman straight in the eye, as his tear ducts produce two shiny bubbles, and says, "You're right. It is cleaner.." Adirondacks it is, Freeman.

I. NEPHELOMETER: An instrument for measuring or registering the amount of cloudiness in a given area.

A panicked Matt Clarksdale scrambles after them as they head toward the shuttle van with a spring to their steps. Clarksdale pleads, "Wait, Mr. Leedskalnin... WAIT! What do we do now? Where do we go?" "You were in the auditorium, weren't you?" Al asks, "Go home to your loved ones and do the things you want to do. Say the things you want to say. It' a whole new game for you kids, for Christ sakes! Just do the right thing from here on out!" The 200 plus geeks gather around the van. "You'll figure it out, and hopefully you won't screw it up!" Al says to them. Dusting himself off, he puts one thin leg in the van, then the other, and says, "Oh... and one last thing folks. Before we all get out of here... there are **NO** aliens! I repeat, **NO** aliens. In fact, there's no such thing as an alien to the cosmos, just untold billions of varied life forms and species thriving throughout the universe. That's right! There are **BILLIONS** of other life forms, and the universe is teeming with them! Now good luck to you all, and good day!"

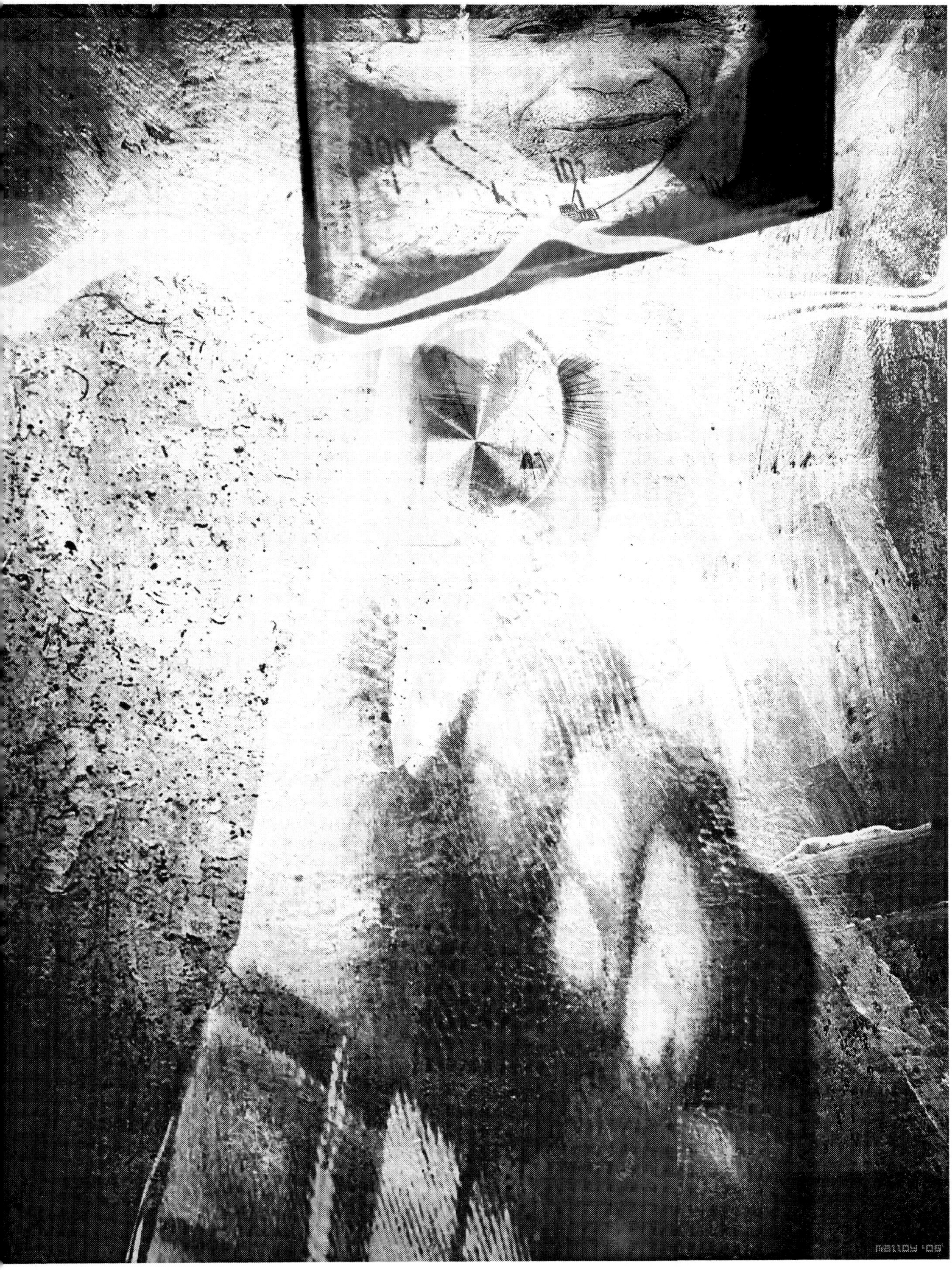
malloy '08

Peabody revs the van in neutral as they slowly roll off the plain. They drive through the throng of overnight campers, each of them gently waving as the shuttle van passes by. They wave as if Al and Peabody were the new messiahs on their way out of the valley, to deliver the message that it's going to be ok, that the world must now stop, and that the humans must now slow down whether they like it or not. But nothing could be further from their minds. Al and Peabody are already onto the next thing, knowing that the earth is saf for at least a moment, hopefully, for a lifetime. They no longer have the foreboding burden they've lived with for so long, and as a result have actually become inexplicably inter-twined. That's the only truth Al knows. It's because he's a Montauk Baby, and in his own way, so is Peabody.

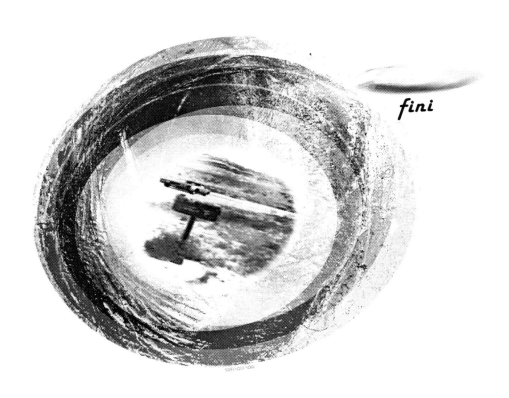

fini

"IN THE WORDS OF AL LEEDSKALNIN" 7 things

1. there are infinite types of "aliens", so many that it would be ridiculous to categorize and or analyze them

2. We are also completely defenseless in front of millions of years of advanced technology and the understanding of time and matter and so forth, we have absolutely no control over anything but ourselves.

3. truth is, the alien's themselves don't know who or what god is, they don't even know from where they come from let alone where we come from. They are aeons removed from their origins just as we are. they are quite fascinated with the emotions of humans. Others, like the Ea are more advanced in many ways but not necessarily older.

4. Soon, very soon, the past present and future will all merge into a finite point and no—one and I mean NO-ONE knows what the outcome will be. We do know that there are good and there are malevolent intelligences involved that are both most concerned and motivated by their own needs of survival.

5. The current reality continues to mask the banality of existence with false exuberance compelled by technology to the deterioration of the logos (Al channeling an elemental)

6. Hell and a Handbasket!   They should all be in baby diapers with lollipops to suck on all day.

7. what's happening is not only is perceived time moving too fast, technology itself is moving too fast and is completely out of control but more importantly the novelty of all things human is coming to an end

Peabody Freeman, July 31, 2017

headfood

http://deoxy.org/t_adt.htm

www.johnjayharper.com

www.phenomena.cinescape.com

http://www.aztlan.net/rumblings_center_galaxy.htm

www.brucelipton.com

www.wolflodge.org

www.thegreatyear.com

www.lorencoleman.com

http://www.zayra.de/soulcom/pinealwww.shamansdrum.org

www.shamanlinks.net

www.gizapyramid.com

www.awakeninthedream.com

www.levity.com/alchemy/texts.htm

http://diseyes.lycaeum.org/index.htm

http://fusionanomaly.net/montauk.htm

http://www.expansions.com/main

http://www.bielek.com/stewart.htm

http://www.philadelphia-experiment.com/Stewart_Swerdlow.htm

http://educate-yourself.org/ab/abglobalscienceinteviewaug97.shtm

http://www.crystalinks.com/montauk.htm

notes

notes

notes

notes

notes

notes

notes

notes

notes

notes

Printed in the United States
62546LVS00004B